# The
# Lantern of the
# Path

# The Lantern of the Path

Imam Ja`far Al-Sadiq

translated by
Shaykh Fadhlalla Haeri
&
Muna Bilgrami

Zahra Publications

# Zahra Publications

**Third edition published jointly by**
Element Books and Zahra Publications in 2004

© 2018, Zahra Publications
**Distributed & Republished in 2018**
**Publisher: Zahra Publications**
www.sfhfoundation.com
www.zahrapublications.com

Designed and typeset in South Africa by
Quintessence Publishing
Cover Design by Quintessence Publishing

Set in 11 point on 15 point, Palatino Linotype
Printed and bound by Lightning Source

ISBN (Printed Version); Paperback: 978-1-928329-09-1

# Table of Contents

# Book Description

---

*The Lantern of The Path* comprises ninety-nine chapters. Each one is a threshold to the next, guiding the reader through the broad spectrum of ageless wisdom, like a lantern along the path of reality. The author illuminates the inner meanings of outer practices which range from practical everyday acts of behavior, to the practices of worship, morals and ethics, and the pillars of religion.

Practical and profound, this concise volume is a useful guide for those who wish to cultivate their inner being.

# About the Author

Imam Ja`far Al-Sadiq is the sixth Imam in the line of the Twelve Imams descended from the Prophet Muhammad, Imam Ja`far ibn Muhammad al-Sādiq (702–765 C.E. or 17th Rabi` al-Awwal 83 AH – 15th Shawwal 148 AH) was the founder of the Ja`fari School of Islamic Law and a renowned scholar of his age. His father was the Imam Muhammad al-Baqir and his mother, Farwa, was a great-granddaughter of Abu Bakr. He lived in Arabia in the eighth century. He devoted his attention to interpreting divine utterances and applied himself to such controversial subjects as *irādah* (free will) and *qadr* (the power to direct one's own actions). He is regarded as one of the greatest of the imams and is also revered by the Naqshbandi Sunni Sufi chain.

Before his imamate he lived through the last twelve years of his grandfather's and nineteen of his father's imamate. His lifetime spanned the rule of the last few caliphs of the Umayyad and the first two of the Abbasid dynasties. Whilst he did not overtly contest their secular leadership, he was, as were all the Imams to even greater or lesser degrees, persecuted by them.

Despite living at a time of tumultuous political change, the Imam was at the crest of the peak of intellectual activity that had developed by them. Much controversy and discussion had arisen over such issues as free-will and compulsion, speculative theology and philosophical enlightenment. These and other related issues in the Islamic sciences occupied the forefront of scholarly life and it was the Imam who clarified and resolved many points; for example, he identified the answer to the conflict between free-will and compulsion as falling between the two extremes. It was also he who delineated the guideline of using the Qur'an to validate prophetic traditions: if they were in agreement they could be accepted, if not, they were rejected. The depth and breadth of his knowledge of the traditions, their authentication and exposition, was unmatched by any of his contemporaries.

His profound spiritual inheritance and teachings magnetized scores of students and seekers of true knowledge: at least four thousand are known to have taken knowledge from him. Among those who considered him their master were the founders of two of the main remaining schools of Islamic Law, Abu Hanifa and Malik ibn Anas, and Jabir ibn Hayyan, founder of Arab alchemy, whose teachings greatly influenced the later physician-philosophers al-Razi (Rhazes), Avicenna and Miskawayh.

The nickname he is most often known by, al-Sadiq, meaning 'the truthful', reflects the love both Sunnis and Shi`ahs alike had for him. The Caliph al-Mansur, however, disliked intensely the Imam's popularity and influence, though he paid lip-service to him. The Imam died in 148/765, naming beforehand as the successor to the imamate his son, Musa al-Kathim. The Isma`ili sect of Shi`ah Islam originated at his death by the Isma`ilis' assumption that the imamate would automatically transfer to his dead son, Isma`il. The rest of the Shi`ah followed the Imam's will in acknowledging Musa as their seventh Imam.

# About
# Shaykh Fadhlalla Haeri

Shaykh Fadhlalla Haeri is a spiritual philosopher and writer whose role as a teacher grew naturally out of his own quest for self-fulfillment. Since childhood he has been attracted to scientific investigation and intellectual pursuit. He was born in Karbala, Iraq, and is a descendant of several generations of well-known and revered spiritual leaders.

After a stint in industry and consulting, he embarked on teaching, writing and meditating.

His awareness of global realpolitik compelled him to seek a truth that would reconcile the past with the present, the East and West. His discovery affirms that One Cosmic Reality is the source behind all known and unknown states.

Shaykh Haeri's unifying perspective emphasizes practical, actionable knowledge of self-transformation. It provides a natural bridge between different approaches to spirituality, offering common ground of higher knowledge for various religions, sects and secular outlooks.

His main work has been to make traditional Islamic teachings more comprehensible and widely available to the modern seeker through courses and publications. Shaykh Fadhlalla Haeri is currently engaged in lecturing and writing books and commentaries on the Holy Qur'an and related subjects, with particular emphasis on ethics, self-development and gnosis (*'irfan*).

# Acknowledgment

---

Zahra Publications is grateful to the sponsors of this book and to those people who arranged for the reprinting of this book. Muna Haeri Bilgrami for her editorial input and for her translation of the text. To Michael Mann for believing in the message and the project.

We are grateful to all the above individuals and those many unmentioned for bringing this important book to publication.

# Introduction

The path of Islam contains a most comprehensive and total system of conduct for the wayfarer. The outer behavior of a true Muslim reflects what is deep in his inner consciousness.

As creation is based on unity, *tawhīd* as it is called in Arabic, every aspect of human experience reflects an aspect of unity. The Muslim is he who has submitted and surrendered in peace and knowledge to this wholesome and naturally balanced ecology. The outer courtesy of behavior emanates from an inner equilibrium. Outer certainty emanates from inner submission and contentment. Outer nobility and courage emanate from inner awareness of the immense mercy and compassion of the Creator.

The outer behavior, courtesies, practices and rituals of Islam are all manifestations of a subtler and finer inner conditioning, and the balanced fusion of the outer and the inner in the journey of this world. If there is an inner attribute there must be a corresponding, outer expression which is a symptom of an inner attribute.

In his teachings, Imam Ja`far al-Sadiq shows the way to equilibrium in a most inspired way of *tawhīd*. As a man of insight and knowledge he sees the unified hand and demonstrates it to the sincere seeker. These teachings can be of benefit to anyone who has an interest in spiritual matters and is concerned with benefiting from the path of

Islam.

The Imam's explanations in *'The Lantern of The Path'* contain many levels of understanding. Much depends upon the state of the seeker and the extent of his sincerity. Although this book is small, its meanings are vast. We pray to Allah to increase our knowledge and experience of His vast compassion and mercy.

**Shaykh Fadhlalla Haeri**

# Publisher's Note

---

Though there can be no doubt as to the truth and authenticity of the teachings contained in this book, it should be mentioned that there is some controversy over whether this book was penned by the Imam himself. Both Allamah Majlisi and Allamah Hurr al-Amili felt that the book's division into ninety-nine chapters and its emphasis on inner meanings is a style more suited to the gnostic, or Sufi scholars. Other scholars, however, affirm that this is the work of the Imam, among them al-Sayyid Ali ibn Tawus, Shaykh al-Kaf`ami, and al-Shahid al-Thani. In the absence of unanimity, we can only say that 'The Lantern of The Path' is generally attributed to Imam Ja`far al-Sadiq.

# Translator's Note and Acknowledgments

This small and simple book was most difficult and complex to translate. The translation began years ago by my father, Shaykh Fadhlalla Haeri, when he translated *'The Lantern of The Path'* during some discourses. Though the task then fell to me to coordinate and execute the final translation, it was not without the considerable help of several scholars that the final version was achieved. A formal translation was first done by Aisha Abdar-Rahman Al-Tarjumana. Both hers and Shaykh Fadhlalla's versions were used in translating it anew, throughout which Dr Syed Mohsin Muzaffar Naqvi helped in unearthing the meanings of obscure words and phrases. This translation was subsequently reviewed and edited by both Asadullah adh-Dhakir Yate and Christopher Flint. I am deeply grateful to all of them, not least for all that I learnt in the process, especially from my father. I sincerely hope that for those who read *'The Lantern of The Path'*, it will open up inner delights, as it has done for me.

**Muna H. Bilgrami**

# CHAPTER I
# Bondage ( `ubudiyah)

The roots of conduct have four aspects: conduct with God, conduct with the self, conduct with creation (i.e. people), and conduct with this world. Each of these aspects is based upon seven principles, just as there are seven principles of conduct with God: giving Him His due, keeping His limits, being thankful for His gift, being content with His decree, being patient with His trials, glorifying His sanctity, and yearning for Him.

The seven principles of conduct with the self are fear, striving, enduring harm, spiritual discipline, seeking truthfulness and sincerity, withdrawing the self from what it loves, and binding it in poverty (*faqr*).

The seven principles of conduct with creation are forbearance, forgiveness, humility, generosity, compassion, good counsel, justice and fairness.

The seven principles of conduct with this world are being content with what is at hand, preferring what is available to what is not, abandoning the quest for the elusive, hating overabundance, choosing abstinence (*zuhd*), knowing the evils of this world and abandoning any desire for it, and negating its dominance. When all these qualities are found in one person, he is then one of God's elites, one of His close bondsmen and friends (*awliya'*).

# CHAPTER 2
## More on Bondage

Bondage is an essence, the inner nature of which is lordship (*rububiyah*). Whatever is missing in bondage is found in lordship, and whatever is veiled from lordship is found in bondage.

As God said:

✿ We will soon show them Our signs in the universe and in their own souls, until it will become quite clear to them that it is the truth. Is it not sufficient as regards your Lord that He is a witness over all things? (41:53)

This means He exists both in your absence and in your presence.

Bondage means ridding oneself of everything, and the way to obtain this is to deny the self what it desires and to make it bear what it dislikes. The key to this is abandoning rest, loving seclusion and following the path of recognition of the need for God. The Prophet said, 'Worship God as if you see Him, Even if you do not see Him, He sees you.'

The letters of the Arabic word for 'bondsman' (`abd) are three: `ayn, ba' and dāl. The `ayn is one's knowledge (`ilm) of God. The *ba'* is one's distance (*bawn*) from other than Him, and the *dāl* is one's nearness (*dunuw*) to God with the restriction of neither contingent qualities nor veil.

The principles of conduct have four aspects, as we mentioned at the beginning of the first chapter.

# CHAPTER 3
# On Lowering the Gaze

There is nothing more gainful than lowering one's gaze, for the sight is not lowered from things which God has forbidden unless the witnessing of majesty and glory has already come to the heart.

The Commander of the Faithful was asked what could help in lowering one's gaze. He said, 'Submission to the power of Him Who is aware of your secret. The eye is the spy of the hearts and the messenger of the intellect; therefore lower your gaze from whatever is not appropriate to your faith, from whatever your heart dislikes and from whatever your intellect finds repugnant.'

The Prophet said, 'Lower your eyes and you will see wonders.'

God said:

✣ Say to the believing men that they cast down their looks and guard their private parts. (24:30)

Jesus said to the disciples, 'Beware of looking at forbidden things, for that is the seed of desire and leads to deviant behavior.'

John the Baptist said, 'I would prefer death to a glance

which is unnecessary.'

`Abdallah ibn Mas`ud said to a man who had visited a woman while she was ill, 'It would have been better for you to lose your eyes than to have visited your sick person.'

Whenever the eye looks at something forbidden, a knot of desire is tied in the person's heart, and that knot will only be united by one of two conditions: either by weeping out of grief and regret in true repentance, or by taking possession of what one desired and looked at. And if a person takes possession unjustly, without repentance, then that will take him to the Fire. As for the one who repents of it with grief and regret, his abode is the Garden and his destiny is God's favor.

# CHAPTER 4
## On Walking

If you are intelligent, then you should be of firm resolution and sincere intention before you set out for any place, for surely the self's nature is to overstep the bounds and encroach on the forbidden. You should reflect when you walk, and take note of the wonders of God's work wherever you go.

Do not be mocking, or strut when you walk; God said:

✿ Do not go about in the land exulting overmuch.
(31:18)

Lower your gaze from whatever is inappropriate to faith, and remember God frequently. There is a tradition which says that those places where, and in connection with which, God is mentioned will testify to that before God on the Day of Judgment and will ask forgiveness for those people so that God will let them enter the Garden.

Do not speak excessively with people along the way, for that is bad manners. Most of the roads are the traps and markets of Satan, so do not feel safe from his tricks. Make your coming and your going in obedience to God, striving for His pleasure, for all your movements will be recorded in your book,[1]

> as God said:

> ✿ On the day when their tongues and their hands and their feet shall bear witness against them regarding what they did. (24:24)

and

> ✿ We have made every man's actions to cling to his neck. (17:13)

---

1    i.e. that book in which your good and bad deeds are recorded, to be consulted on the Day of Judgment.

# CHAPTER 5
## On Knowledge

Knowledge is the basis of every sublime state and the culmination of every high station. That is why the Prophet said, 'It is the duty of every Muslim, man and woman, to seek knowledge,' that is, the knowledge of precaution (*taqwa*) and certainty.

Imam `Ali said, 'Seek knowledge, though it be in China,' meaning the knowledge of gnosis of the self – in it is contained knowledge of the Lord.

The Prophet said, 'Whoever knows his own self knows his Lord; moreover, you should acquire that knowledge without which no action is correct, and that is sincerity... We seek refuge with God from knowledge which has no benefit', that is, from knowledge which is contrary to actions performed with sincerity. Know that a small amount of knowledge requires a great deal of action, because knowledge of the Hour[2] requires the person who has such knowledge to act accordingly during his entire life.

Jesus said, 'I saw a stone on which was written, "Turn me over", so I turned it over. Written on the other side was

---

2       All will come to an end and every moment of life will be questioned.

"Whoever does not act by what he knows will be doomed by seeking what he does not know, and his own knowledge will be turned against him."'

God revealed to David, 'The least that I shall do to someone with knowledge who does not act by his knowledge is worse than the seventy inner punishments which result in My removing from his heart the sweetness of My remembrance.'

There is no way to God except via knowledge. And knowledge is the adornment of man in this world and the next, his driver to Paradise, and by means of it he attains God's contentment with him.

He who truly knows is the one in whom sound actions, pure supplications, truthfulness and precaution speak out; not his tongue, his debates, his comparisons, assertions or claims. In times other than these, those who sought knowledge were those who had intellect, piety, wisdom, modesty and caution; but nowadays we see that those who seek it do not have any of these qualities. The man of knowledge needs intellect, kindness, compassion, good counsel, forbearance, patience, contentment and generosity; while anyone wishing to learn needs a desire for knowledge, will, devotion (of his time and energy), piety, caution, memory and resolution.

# CHAPTER 6
## Giving Judgment

Giving judgment is not permissible for someone who has not been endowed by God with the qualities of inner purity, sincerity in both his hidden and visible actions, and a proof from his Lord in every state. This is because whoever has judged has decreed, and decree is only valid by the permission of God and by His proof. Whoever is liberal in his judgment, without having made a proper examination, is ignorant and will be taken to task for his ignorance and will be burdened with his judgment as the tradition indicates. Knowledge is a light which God casts into the heart of whomsoever He wills.

The Prophet said, 'Whoever is boldest among you in judging is also the most insolent to God'. Does not the judge know that he is the one who has come between God and His bondsmen, and that he is wavering between the Garden and the Fire? Sufyan ibn `Uyaynah said, 'How can anyone else benefit from my knowledge if I have denied myself its benefit?' It is inappropriate for anyone to judge on what is permissible (*halāl*) and what is forbidden (*harām*) among creation, except for one who causes the people of his time, his village, and his city to follow the truth through obedience to the Prophet and who recognizes what is applicable of his judgment. The Prophet said, 'It is because giving judgment is such a tremendous affair, in which there is no place for "hopefully", "perhaps" or "may be".'

The Commander of the Faithful said to a judge, 'Do you know the difference between those verses of the Qur'an which abrogate and those which are abrogated?'

'No'.

'Do you have a command of the intentions of God in the parables of the Qur'an?'

'No'.

'Then you have perished and caused others to perish,' the Commander of the Faithful replied.

A judge needs to know the various meanings of the Qur'an, the truth of the Prophetic way, the inward indications, courtesies, consensus and disagreements, and to be familiar with the bases of what they agree upon and disagree about. Then he must have acute discrimination, sound action, wisdom, and precaution. If he has these, things, then let him judge.

# CHAPTER 7
# Enjoining what is Good and Forbidding what is Evil

Whoever has not thrown off his anxieties, been purified of the evils of his self and its appetites, defeated Satan, and entered under the guardianship of God and the security of His protection, cannot properly enjoin what is good and forbid what is evil; and since he has not attained these aforementioned qualities, whatever affair he tackles in attempting to enjoin what is good and forbid what is evil will be a proof against him, and people will not benefit from it.

God said:

☼ What! Do you enjoin men to be good and neglect your own souls? (2:44)

Anyone who does that is called upon thus: Oh traitor! Do you demand from My creation that which you have rejected for yourself and have slackened the reins [in this regard] upon yourself?

It is related that Tha`labah al-Asadi asked the Messenger of God about this verse:

☼ O you who believe! Take care of your souls;

he who errs cannot hurt you when you are on the right way. (5:105)

The Messenger of God said, 'Enjoin what is good and forbid what is evil, and be forbearing in whatever afflicts you, until such time when you see meanness obeyed and passions followed, and when everyone will have conceit about their own opinion, then you should concern yourself only with yourself, and ignore the affairs of the common people.'

A person who enjoins what is good needs to be knowledgeable about what is permissible and what is forbidden; he must be free from his personal inclinations regarding what he enjoins and forbids, give good counsel to people, be merciful and compassionate to them, and call them with gentleness in a very clear manner, while recognizing their different characters so that he can put each in his proper place.

He must see the intrigues of the self and the machinations of Satan. He must be patient in whatever befalls him, and must not seek compensation from people for that which he instructs them in, nor complain about them. He should not make use of vehemence or passion. He should not become angry for his own sake. He should make his intention purely for God, and seek His help and desire Him. But if people oppose him and are harsh to him, he must be patient; and if they agree with him and accept his verdict, he must be thankful, entrusting his affair to God and looking to his own faults.

# CHAPTER 8
# How the Men of Knowledge are Ruined

Caution and fear are the legacy of knowledge and its measure; knowledge is the ray of gnosis and the heart of belief. Whoever is denied caution is not a man of knowledge, even if he can split hairs in dealing with obscure items of knowledge.

God said:

✧ Only those of His servants who are possessed of knowledge fear Allah. (35:28)

Men of knowledge are ruined by eight things: greed and miserliness, showing off and partisanship, love of praise, delving into things whose reality they cannot reach, affectation by taking excessive pains to beautify their speech with superfluous expressions, lack of modesty before God, boastfulness, and not acting upon what they know.

Jesus said, 'The most wretched of all people is he who is known for his knowledge, not for his actions.'

The Prophet said, 'Do not sit with every presumptuous caller who summons you from certainty to doubt, from sincerity to showing off, from humility to pride, from good counsel to enmity, and from abstinence to desire. Draw near to the person with knowledge, who summons you from pride to humility, from showing off to sincerity, from doubt to certainty, from desire to abstinence, from enmity to good counsel.' None are fit to preach to creation except that person who has gone beyond these evils by his truthfulness. He sees the faults of speech and knows what is sound from what is unsound, the defectiveness of thoughts, and the temptations of the self and his fancies.

`Ali said, 'Be like the kind, compassionate doctor who places the remedy where it will be of benefit.'

They asked Jesus, 'With whom shall we sit, O Spirit of God?'

'With one the sight of whom reminds you of God,' he replied, 'and whose speech increases you in knowledge, and whose actions make you desire the next world.'

# CHAPTER 9
# Guarding Oneself (*ri`ayah*)

W hoever guards his heart from heedlessness, protects
his self from appetites and guards his intellect from
ignorance, will be admitted into the company of the vigilant.
Then he who guards his knowledge from fancies, his faith
from innovation, and his properly from the forbidden is
among the righteous.

The Messenger of God said, 'It is a duty for every
Muslim, man and woman, to seek knowledge,' that is,
knowledge of the self. Therefore it is necessary for the self to
be in all states either expressing his gratitude or proffering
his excuse for lack of gratitude. If this is acceptable to God
it is a favor upon him, and if not it is justice upon him. For
every self it is necessary to work that it may succeed in
its acts of obedience, and for its protection in its efforts to
abstain from doing harm.

The basis of all this is recognition of total need and
dependence on God, caution and obedience. The key to it
is in delegating your affair to God, cutting off expectation
by always remembering death, and seeing that you are
standing in the presence of the All-compelling. This gives
you rest from confinement, rescue from the enemy, and
peace for the self. The means to sincerity in obedience is
harmony, and the root of that rests upon considering life

as being only as long as a day.

The Messenger of God said, 'This world lasts but an hour, so spend it in obedience to God.' The door to all of this is always to withdraw from the world by means of constant reflection. The means to this withdrawal is contentment, and abandoning such existential matters as do not concern you. The means to reflection is emptiness [desirelessness], and the buttress of emptiness is abstinence. The completion of abstinence is precaution, and the door to precaution is fear. The proof of fear is glorification of God, adherence to obeying His commands with sincerity, fear and caution, and holding back from the forbidden; and the guide to this is knowledge.

Almighty God said:

✿ Those of His servants who are possessed of knowledge fear Allah. (35:28)

# CHAPTER 10
# Thankfulness

With every breath you take, a thanksgiving is incumbent upon you – indeed, a thousand thanks or more. The lowest level of gratitude is to see that the blessing comes from God irrespective of the cause for it, and without the heart being attached to that cause. It consists of being satisfied with what is given; it means not disobeying Him with regard to His blessing, or opposing Him in any of His commands and prohibitions because of His blessing. Be a grateful bondsman to God (*abd-Allah*) in every way, and you will find that God is a generous Lord in every way. If there were a way of worshipping God for His sincerest bondsman to follow more excellent than giving thanks at every instance, He would have ascribed to them the name of this worship above the rest of creation. Since there is no form of worship better than that, He has singled out this kind of worship from other kinds of worship, and has singled out those who practice this kind of worship, saying:

✿ Very few of my servants are grateful. (34:13)

Complete thankfulness is to sincerely repent your inability to convey the least amount of gratitude, and expressing this by means of your sincere glorification of God. This is because fitting thanks is itself a blessing bestowed upon the bondsman for which he must also give thanks; it is of greater merit and of a higher state than the original blessing which caused him to respond with thanks in the first place. Therefore, every time one gives thanks one is obliged to give yet greater thanks, and so on ad infinitum, and this while absorbed in His blessings and unable to achieve the ultimate state of gratitude. For how can the bondsman match with gratitude the blessings of God, and when will he match his own action with God's while all along the bondsman is weak and has no power whatsoever, except from God?

God is not in need of the obedience of His bondsmen, for He has the power to increase blessings forever. Therefore be a grateful bondsman to God, and in this manner you will see wonders.

# CHAPTER II
# On Leaving your Home

When you leave your home, do it as if you will never return. Leave only for the sake of obedience to God or for the sake of the faith. Remain tranquil and dignified in your bearing, and remember God both secretly and openly.

One of the companions of Abu Dharr asked a member of Abu Dharr's household where he was and she said, 'He has gone out.' When the man asked when Abu Dharr would return, she replied, 'When he returns is in the hands of someone else,' for he has no power on his own.

Learn from God's creation, both the pious and the deviants, wherever you go. Ask God to place you among His sincere and truthful bondsmen, and to join you to those of them who have passed on and to gather you in their company. Praise Him, and give thanks for the appetites He has made you avoid, and the ugly actions of the wrongdoers from which He has protected you. Lower your gaze from carnal appetites and forbidden things, and pursue the right course on your journey. Be vigilant, fearing God at every step, as if you were crossing the straight path. Do not be distracted. Offer a greeting to His people, both giving it first and answering with it. Give help to those who ask for it in a righteous cause, guide those who are lost and ignore the ignorant.

When you return to your home, enter it as a corpse enters the grave, its only concern being to receive the mercy and forgiveness of God.

# CHAPTER 12
# On Reciting the Qur'an

---

Whoever recites the Qur'an and does not humble himself before God, whose heart is not softened, nor regret and fear provoked within him, undervalues the immensity of God's affair and is in a clear state of loss.

The person who recites the Qur'an needs three things: a fearful heart, a tranquil and receptive body, and an appropriate place to recite. When his heart fears God, then the accursed Satan flees from him,

As God said:

☼ When you recite the Qur'an, seek refuge with Allah from the accursed Shaytan. (16:98)

When he frees himself of all attachments, then his heart is devoted to recitation, and nothing impedes him from obtaining the blessing of the light of the Qur'an and its benefits. When he finds an empty place and withdraws from people, having acquired the two qualities of humility of heart and tranquility of body, then his soul and his innermost being will feel communion with God, and he will discover the sweetness of how God speaks to His right-acting bondsmen, how He shows His gentleness, to them and singles them out for all the varieties of His marks of honor and wondrous signs. If he drinks a cup of this drink, he will never prefer any other state to this nor any other moment to this. He will prefer this to every act of obedience and devotion, since it contains intimate conversation with the Lord without any intermediary.

So beware of how you read the Book of your Lord, the guardian to whom you aspire, how you respond to His commands and avoid His prohibitions, and how you observe His limits, for it is a mighty Book:

> ✪ Falsehood shall not come to it from before it nor from behind it, a revelation from the Wise, the Praised One. (41:42)

Therefore recite it in an orderly manner and contemplatively, and adhere to the limits of His promise and His threat. Reflect on its examples and warnings. Beware of paying undue respect to the recitation of its letters while failing to observe the legal limits contained therein.

# CHAPTER 13
## Dress

The best adornment of the believer's garment is precaution and the most blessed garment is belief. As God said:

> ☼ And clothing that guards [against evil]; that is best. (7:26)

Outward dress is a blessing from God in order to preserve the modesty of the sons of Adam; it is a mark of honor which God has given to the descendants of Adam. He did not give that honor to any other creature; it is given to the believers as a means of carrying out their obligations. Your best garments are those which do not distract you from God – those garments, in fact, which bring you closer to remembrance of Him, and gratitude and obedience to Him, They do not, however, move you to pride, conceit, pretence, boastfulness or arrogance: those things are the scourge of the faith, and their legacy is hardness of heart.

When you put on your clothes, remember that God veils your wrong actions with His mercy. You should clothe your inward part as you clothe your outward part with your garment. Let your inward truth be veiled in awe of God, and let your outward truth be veiled in obedience.

Take heed of the overflowing favor of God, since He created the means to make garments for covering physical immodesty and opened the gates for repentance, regret, and seeking succor, in order to veil the inward parts, and their wrong actions and bad character.

Do not expose anyone's faults when God has concealed worse things in yourself. Occupy yourself with your own faults, and overlook matters and situations which do not concern you. Beware lest you exhaust your life in other people's actions and exchange your irreplaceable endowed wealth with someone else, thereby destroying yourself. Forgetting wrong actions brings about the greatest punishments of God in this world, and is the most ample cause for punishment in the next. So long as the bondsman occupies himself with obeying God, with recognizing his own faults and leaving alone whatever might devalue faith in God, he is spared ruin and is immersed in the sea of God's mercy, attaining the gems and the benefits of wisdom and clarity. But as long as he forgets his own wrong actions, is ignorant of his own faults, and falls back on his power and strength, he will never be successful.

# CHAPTER 14
## Showing Off

---

D o not show off your actions to someone who neither gives life nor causes death, and who cannot take away from you your burdens. Showing off is a tree whose only fruit is hidden association of other gods with God, and its root is hypocrisy. The vain one will be told on the Day of Judgment, 'Take what you consider to be the reward of your actions from those you took as your partners with Me. Look to those whom you worshipped and called on, from whom you entertained hopes and whom you feared. And know that you cannot conceal anything inside of you from God: you will be deceived by yourself.'

God said:

✣ They desire to deceive Allah and those who believe, and they deceive only themselves and they do not perceive. (2:9)

Showing off most frequently occurs in the way people glance at others, speak, eat, drink, arrive somewhere, sit with others, dress, laugh, and in the way they perform prayers, pilgrimage, *jihad*[3], recitation of the Qur'an, and all outward acts of devotion.

However, he who is sincere towards God, who fears Him in his heart, and who sees himself as lacking even after he has exerted himself with every effort, will find that God is contented with him as a result, and he will be among those whom one expects to be free from showing off and hypocrisy, provided he continues to be in that state.

---

3      The Arabic term *jihad*, usually translated into European languages as holy war, more on the basis of its juridical usage in Islam rather than on its much more universal meaning in the Qur'an and Hadith, is derived from the root *jhd* whose primary meaning is to strive or to exert oneself. *Jihad* is a means of inner purification and freedom, and an outer defense of the way of God.

# CHAPTER 15
# Truthfulness

Truthfulness is a light which radiates its reality in its own world: it is like the sun, from whose reality everything seeks light without any decrease occurring in this reality. A truthful person, in fact, is a man who believes every liar, due to the reality of his own truthfulness. It means that nothing which is opposed to truthfulness, nothing, even, which is not truthfulness, is permitted to coexist with it; just as happened with Adam, who believed Iblis when he lied because Iblis had sworn a false oath to him and there was no lying in Adam.

God said:

☼ We did not find in him any determination. (20:115)

because Iblis originated something previously unknown, both outwardly and inwardly. Iblis will be gathered with his lie, and he will never benefit from the truthfulness of Adam.

Yet it benefited Adam that he believed the lie of Iblis, as God testified for him when He said that he was not constant in what was contrary to his custom. This really means that his being chosen was not at all diminished by Satan's lies.

Truthfulness is the attribute of the truthful. The reality of truthfulness demands that God purify His bondsman, as He mentioned regarding the truthfulness of Jesus on the Day of Reckoning. He indicated it by referring to the guiltlessness of the truthful men of the community of Muhammad, saying:

> ✿ This is the day when their truth shall benefit the truthful ones. (5:119)

The Commander of the Faithful[4] said, 'Truthfulness is the sword of God in His heaven and earth: it cuts everything it touches.' If you want to know whether you are truthful or lying, then look into the truthfulness of what you mean and the conclusion of your claim. Then gauge them both according to a scale from God, as if you were present on the Day of Resurrection. God said:

> ✿ And measuring out on that day will be just. (7:8)

If there is balance and harmony in what you mean, then your claim is successful, and your truthfulness is in the fact that the tongue does not differ from the heart, nor the heart from the tongue. The truthful person with this description is like the angel who draws out his soul; if the soul is not drawn out, then what is it to do?

---

4      Imam `Ali.

# CHAPTER 16
## Sincerity

Sincerity lies in all distinguished actions; it is a notion that starts with acceptance and ends with God's pleasure. Therefore he whose actions God accepts and with whom He is content is the sincere one, even if his actions are few. Whoever does not have his actions accepted is not sincere, even if his actions are many, as we can see when we consider what happened with Adam and Iblis, may he be cursed.

The sign of acceptance is the existence of integrity and correctness, by expending all that is desirable with accurate awareness of every movement and stillness. In upholding what he has, the self of the sincere one is consumed, and his life is spent so as to put what he has in order, unifying knowledge and action, the doer and what is done by the action. For if he has attained that, he has attained all, and if he misses it he misses all; and that is brought about by purifying the meanings of disassociation (*tanzih*) in His unity. As the first Imam said, 'Those who act will perish, except for those who worship; those who worship will perish except for those who know; those who know will perish except for those who are truthful; those who are truthful will perish except for those who are sincere; those who are sincere will perish except for those who have precaution; those who have precaution will perish except for those who have certainty, and those who have certainty are of exalted character.'

As God said:

✡ And serve your Lord until there comes to you that which is certain. (15:99)

The lowest level of sincerity is when the bondsman exerts himself as much as he can, and then does not consider his action to have any worth with God so that he does not make his Lord recompense him for his actions according to his knowledge, for if God asks him to fulfill the full duties of slavehood (`ubudiyah`) he would be unable to do so. The lowest station of the sincere person in the world is safety from all wrong actions, to be rescued from the Fire and to win the Garden in the next world.[5]

---

5    If the slave parades his good deeds and expects acknowledgment, God could hold him to account as to whether he has fulfilled his obligations completely; and no one, therefore, can beware.

# CHAPTER 17
# Precaution

---

Precaution (*taqwa*) has three facets:

1. Precaution by dependence on God, which means leaving behind contradiction and going beyond any shade of doubt, and this is the precaution exercised by the highest.

2. The precaution of God, which means to abandon all doubtful matters and to leave the forbidden (*harām*) alone; this is the precaution of the elite.

3. The precaution of the Fire and Punishment, which results in leaving alone what is forbidden; this is the precaution of the general public.

Precaution is like water flowing in a river. The three levels of precaution are like trees of every color and variety planted on the bank of that river, each tree absorbing water from that river according to its essence, capacity, delicateness and thickness. Then the benefits which creatures take from these trees and fruits are according to their value and worth.

God said:

✿ Palm trees having one root and [others] having distinct roots – they are watered with one water, and We make some of them excel others in fruit. (13:4)

Precaution in acts of obedience to God is like water for the trees, and the natures of the trees and their fruits in their colors and tastes are like the measures of belief. Whoever has the highest degree in belief and the purest nature with respect to the soul has the greatest precaution. He who is precautions has the purer and more sincere worship: whoever is like that is nearer to God. But every act of devotion that is founded on something other than precaution comes to nothing.

God said:

✿ Is he, therefore, better who laid his foundation on fear of Allah and [His] good pleasure, or he who laid his foundation on the edge of a cracking, hollowed bank, so it broke down with him into the fire of Hell? (9:109)

The explanation of precaution is to avoid entering an affair which contains no harm simply out of fear of one which does. It is, in reality, obedience without rebellion, remembrance without forgetfulness, knowledge without ignorance, and it is accepted by God and not rejected.

# CHAPTER 18
## Godfearingness

Close the gates of your limbs and senses to all that will harm your heart, remove your standing with God, and bring in its wake grief and regret on the Day of Judgment and shame about the evil actions you committed.

The scrupulous person must have three principles: he should overlook the faults of all people, he should avoid offending them, and he should balance censure with praise.

The basis of Godfearingness is constantly to take the self to account, to be truthful in one's words and pure in one's transactions, to leave every doubtful thing, to abandon every defect and doubt, to separate oneself from all which does not concern you and not to open doors which you will not know how to close. Do not sit with anyone who obscures what is clear for you, nor with someone who takes the faith lightly. Do not question knowledge which your heart has no capacity for, and which you will not understand, of whoever said it, and cut off anyone who cuts you off from God.

# CHAPTER 19
## Social Interactions

Courteous social relations with God's creation while avoiding all acts of disobedience to Him is a sign of God's excessive generosity with His bondsman. Whoever is sincere and humble before God in his innermost being will have good social interaction externally.

Keep company with people for the sake of God and do not keep company merely for your own share of worldly affairs, for seeking rank, showing off, or for reputation. Do not fall below the limits of the *shari`ah* for the sake of social intercourse, such as trying to keep up with others, or gaining a reputation, for these things cannot make up for you, and you will miss the next world, with no recourse. Treat someone who is older than you as you would your father, someone who is younger than you as you would a son. Treat your peer as you would a brother. Do not abandon what you know to be certain within yourself for something heard from other people which you doubt. Be gentle when you enjoin good and compassionate when you forbid evil. Never abandon good counsel in any circumstance.

As God said:

✿ Speak to people good words. (2:83)

Cut yourself off from what makes you forget to remember God, when temptation distracts you from obedience to Him, for that comes from the friends and helpers of Satan. Do not allow the sight of them to move you to dissimulation with the truth, for that would be a terrible loss indeed. We seek refuge with Almighty God.

# CHAPTER 20
## Sleep

Sleep the sleep of the mindful; do not sleep the sleep of the heedless. For the mindful among the astute sleep only for rest, and do not purposely sleep through laziness.

The Prophet said, 'My eyes sleep, but my heart does not.' When you go to sleep, have the intention to lighten your burden on the angels and disengage the self from its appetites, and to examine yourself by your sleep; be aware of the fact that you are incapable and weak. You have no power over any of your movements and stillnesses, except by the judgment and measure of God.

Know that sleep is the brother of death. Use it as a guide to death, for there is no way to wake up in death or to return to correct action once you have missed it. Whoever sleeps through an obligatory, recommended or supererogatory prayer is at fault, and his sleep is the sleep of the heedless and the path of the losers; he is at fault. Whoever sleeps after he has discharged his duties concerning obligatory and recommended prayers, and has carried out his responsibilities, sleeps a praiseworthy sleep. I do not know of anything that is safer than sleep for the people of our times who have attained these qualities: this is because people have ceased to guard their faith and to take care in observing their conduct. They have taken the left-hand path. When a sincere bondsman strives not to speak out of place, how can he avoid hearing that which would prevent him from not speaking unless there is a safeguard? Sleep is one such safeguard.

As God said:

☼ Surely, the hearing and the sight and the heart, all of these shall be questioned about that. (17:36)

In excess sleep there are many evils, even if it is done in the way we have mentioned. Too much sleep is brought about by excess drink, and excess drinking is brought about being excessively satiated. Both of these things weigh heavily on the self to keep it from obedience, and they harden the heart from reflection and humility.

Make your sleep your last affair in this world; remember God with your heart and your tongue. Let your obedience to God overpower your wrongdoings and seek help from Him while you sleep, fasting until the morning prayer, since if you are awakened at night, Satan whispers to you, 'Sleep again, you still have a long night,' for he wants you to miss the time of intimate contemplation and exposure of your state before your Lord. Do not be distracted in seeking forgiveness at dawn, for at that time there is much yearning for those in devoted supplication.

# CHAPTER 21
# Pilgrimage

If you intend to go on pilgrimage, before resolving on it devote your heart to God, stripping it of every preoccupation and every barrier between you and God. Entrust all your affairs to your Creator; rely on Him in all your actions and moments of stillness. Surrender to His decree, decision and judgment. Abandon this world, repose, and all creation. Perform those duties which you are bound to fulfill for other people. Do not rely on your provisions, the animal you ride, your companions, your food, your youth nor your wealth, for fear that they will become your enemies and be harmful to you; in this way you will realize that there is no power, no strength, nor might except by the guardianship of God and His granting of success.

Prepare for the pilgrimage as someone who does not hope to return. Keep good company, and be diligent in observing all your obligations to God and the prophetic practices. Take care to show courtesy, endurance, patience, thankfulness, compassion, and generosity, always putting others before yourself at all times, even those who reject you. Then perform an ablution with the water of sincere repentance for wrong actions; put on the robe of truthfulness, purity, humility and fear. By donning the garments of pilgrimage,[6] withhold yourself from everything which hinders you from remembering God, or that will impede you from showing obedience to Him.

Fulfill His call with an answer whose meaning is clear, pure and sincere when you call on Him, holding on firmly to your belief in Him. Walk around the Ka`bah (*Tawāf*) with your heart along with the angels who walk around the Throne, just as you walk around with the Muslims who go around the Ka`bah. Hasten as you run in flight from your passion, freeing yourself of all your personal assumptions of strength and power. Leave your heedlessness and errors behind when you go out to Mina; do not desire what is unlawful for you and what you do not deserve. Confess your errors at Arafat: set out your contract with God by His Oneness, draw near to Him and fear Him at Muzdalifah. Climb with your soul to the highest assembly when you climb the mountain of Arafat. Slit the throat of passion and greed in the sacrifice. Stone your appetites, baseness, vileness, and blameworthy actions when you stone the Pillar of Aqabah. Shave off your outward and inward faults when you shave your hair. Enter into the security of God, His protection, His veil, His shelter and His watchfulness and abandon the pursuit of your desires by entering the Sacred Precinct. Visit the House, and walk around it to glorify its Master, His wisdom, His majesty and His power. Embrace the Stone, being content with His decree and humble before His might. Leave everything that is other-than-Him in the valedictory *tawāf*. Purify your soul and your innermost being for the meeting with God, on the day when you will meet Him when standing on

---

6    The Arabic here signifies avoidance of anything harmful, as well as putting on the ritual robe of the pilgrim.

Safa', Take on valor and courtesy from God by annihilating your attributes at Marwah. Be consistent in the conditions of your pilgrimage and fulfill the contract you have made with your Lord, by which you will have obliged yourself to Him on the Day of Judgment. Know that God made the pilgrimage obligatory, and singled it out from all the acts of worship in respect of Himself when

He said:

✿ Pilgrimage to the House is incumbent upon people for the sake of Allah; and [upon] everyone who is able to undertake the journey to it. (3:97)

The Prophet established the organization of the rituals of pilgrimage as preparation for, and an indication of, death, the grave, the resurrection and the Day of Judgment. In this lesson for mankind he discriminates between those who will enter the Garden and those who will enter the Fire, through his demonstrating the pilgrimage rites from beginning to end to those with intelligence and prudence.

# CHAPTER 22
## Charity

Obligatory charity[7] for the sake of God is due from every single part of your body, even from every root of your hair. In fact, charity is due for every instant of your life.

Charity of the eye means looking with consideration and averting the gaze from desires and things similar to them. Charity of the ear means listening to the best of sounds, such as wisdom, the Qur'an, the benefits of the faith contained in warnings and good counsel, and to that in which your salvation lies, and by avoiding their opposite, such as lies, slander, and similar things.

Charity of the tongue means to give good counsel to the Muslims, to awaken those who are heedless, and to give abundant glorification and remembrance (*dhikr*), and other, similar things. Charity of the hand means spending money on others, to be generous with God's blessings to you, to use it in writing down knowledge and information by means of which other Muslims will benefit in obedience to God, and to restrain the hand from evil. Charity of the foot means to hasten to carry out one's duty to God

---

7    The Arabic word for charity (*zakāt*) also means something which purifies.

45

by visiting virtuous people, assemblies of remembrance (*dhikr*), putting things right between people, maintaining ties of kinship, engaging in *jihad*, and doing things which will make your heart sound and your faith correct.

We have mentioned here just some of the ways of *zakāt*, namely, those understood by the heart and those the self can deal with; although there are others too numerous to mention, mastered by no one but His sincere and intimate bondsmen. Indeed, these latter are the lords of *zakāt* and to them belongs its mark of distinction. Oh God, give me success in what You love and in what makes You content.

# CHAPTER 23
## Intention

The person who has a sincere intention is the one who has a sound heart; because a sound heart, free from thoughts about forbidden things, comes from making your intention purely for God in all matters.

✧ The day on which neither property will avail, nor sons, except him who comes to Allah with a heart free [from evil]. (26:88-89)

The Prophet said, 'The intention of the believer is better than his action,' and also, 'Actions are by intentions, and every man will obtain what he had intended.' The slave of God must therefore have sincere intention in every moment of action and stillness because then he will not be heedless.

Those who are heedless have been censured by God:
✧ They are nothing but as cattle; nay, they are straying farther off from the path. (25:44)

✧ These are the heedless ones. (7:179)

Intention appears from the heart, according to the purity of knowledge. It varies as belief varies, at different moments in its strength and weakness. The selfishness and passion of those with sincere intention is subjugated to the power of the glorification of God and modesty before Him. He is by his nature, his appetites and his own desires, in a state of discomfort, and yet people find ease at his hand.

# CHAPTER 24
## Remembrance

He who truly remembers God is the one who obeys Him: whoever forgets is disobedient. Obedience is the mark of guidance, disobedience the sign of misguidance. The root of both states lies in remembrance (*dhikr*) and forgetfulness.

Make your heart the focal point of your tongue, which should not move unless the heart indicates, the intellect agrees and your tongue accords with belief. Almighty God knows what you conceal and what you reveal.

Be like someone who has shed his soul from his body, or like someone who is attending the great parade on the Day of Reckoning, not distracting yourself from the obligations which your Lord has laid on you in His commands and prohibitions, His promise and His threat. Do not be occupied with yourself rather than with the duties laid down for you by your Lord.

Wash your heart clean with the water of sorrow and fear; make remembrance of God part of His most glorious remembrance of you. He remembers you, but He does not need you. His remembrance of you is more glorious, more desirable, more praiseworthy, more complete and more ancient than your remembrance of Him.

The knowledge you obtain by His remembrance of you

will beget you humility, modesty and contrition, which will in turn be the cause of your witnessing His nobility and previous, overflowing favor. The latter will then belittle your obedience in your own eyes, however copious it may be as a result of His favors; and you will be sincerely devoted to Him. But your consciousness and esteem of your own remembrance of Him will lead to showing off, pride, foolishness and coarseness in your character, for it means attaching too much importance to your obedience while forgetting His overflowing favor and generosity. It will only make you more distant from Him, and all that you will acquire with the passing of the days is alienation.

There are two sorts of remembrance: sincere remembrance with which the heart is in harmony, and remembrance which arises through banishing any remembrance of other than God. As the Messenger of God said, 'I cannot do justice in properly praising You as You praise Yourself.' The Messenger of God did not set any limit on remembering God, since he knew the truth that God's remembrance of His bondsman was greater than the bondsman's remembrance of Him. Thus it is even more fitting that whoever comes after the Prophet should not set any limits, and whoever wants to remember God should know that as long as God does not remember the bondsman by granting him success in remembering Him, that bondsman will not be able to remember Him.

# CHAPTER 25
# The Ruin of the Reciters

Someone who recites without knowledge is like a vain man who has neither property nor wealth; for people do not hate someone for his lack of possessions, but they detest him for his vanity. He is always at odds with creation in that which is not obligatory upon him, and he who contests creation in what he is not commanded to do is contesting the process of creativity and absolute lordship.

As God said:

☼ Among men is he who disputes in respect of Allah though having no knowledge, nor guidance, nor a book giving light. (31:20)

None will have a harsher punishment than someone who claims a right to the mantle of knowledge without having either the truth or the meaning of it.

Zayd ibn Thabit said to his son, 'My son, do not let God see your name in the register of the vain reciters.' And the Prophet said, 'A time will come for my community in which hearing the name of the man who recites will be considered better than studying, and studying will be considered better than doing the thing with experience...

. The greatest number of hypocrites in my community are among the reciters of the Qur'an.'

Be where the faith recommends you to be, and where you are commanded to be. Conceal your inner state from other people as much as you can. Make your acts of obedience to God have the same relationship as your soul has to your body, so they become an indication of the state you have attained between yourself and your Originator. Seek God's help in all your affairs, and beseech God humbly at the end of the night and at the end of the day.

God said:

✿ Call on your Lord humbly and secretly; surely
He does not love those who exceed the limits. (7:55)

Transgressing is one of the attributes, indeed, one of the hallmarks, of the reciters of our time. Be fearful of God in all your affairs, so that you do not fall into the arena of desire and destroy yourself.

# CHAPTER 26
# Clarification of Truth and Falsehood

Fear God and be where you wish to be among any people you choose to be. There is no conflict for anyone in a state of precaution. Precaution is desirable for all parties; in it is gathered all goodness and maturity. It is the measure of all knowledge and wisdom, of every accepted act of obedience. Precaution is the water which gushes out from the spring of God's gnosis: every branch of knowledge is in need of it. It does not need any confirmation of knowing how to be still in awe of God and His power. Increase in precaution comes from God's acquainting His bondman's secret with His subtle mercy: this is the root of every truth.

Falsehood is whatever cuts you off from God – every group agrees on this also. Therefore avoid falsehood, devoting your secret to God without any attachment.

The Messenger of God said, 'The truest words that the Bedouins spoke are the words of Labid when he said,

Indeed everything but Allah is false

And every blessing is most certainly ephemeral.'

So cling to what is agreed upon by people of purity, piety and precaution in the roots of the faith, the realities of certainty, God's pleasure, and submission. Do not enter into disagreement and disputations among people, for then things will become difficult for you. The chosen community has agreed that God is One and that there is nothing like Him; and that He is just in His judgment, does whatever He wishes, and governs what He wills. One does not ask 'why?' about anything of His making.

There has not been and will never be anything that is not according to His will and desire; He has the power to do what He wills, and He is true in His promise and His threat. The Qur'an is His word, and it existed before phenomenal being, place and time. The creation of phenomenal beings and their annihilation are the same with Him: their creation did not increase His knowledge, nor will their passing decrease His kingdom. His power is mighty and He is majestic, glory be to Him. If someone brings to you anything which falls short of this fundamental truth, do not accept it. Devote your inward being to that and you will see its blessings close at hand. You will be among the victors.

# CHAPTER 27
# The Gnosis of the Prophets

God has provided His Prophets from the treasures of His subtlety, generosity, and mercy. He has taught them from the wealth of His knowledge, and He has singled them out for Himself from among all creation. No one from the entire creation possesses a state or character similar to theirs, for He has made them the means for all creatures to come to Him.

He made obedience to and love for them the cause of His contentment, and opposition lo them and rejection of them a cause for His wrath. He commanded all peoples and groups to follow the religion of their Messenger, rejecting any obedience other than by means of obedience to them, praise of them, recognition of their love, respect and veneration for them, esteem for them and deference to them, and rank with God. Therefore glorify all the prophets of God, and do not place them in the same position as anyone inferior to them. Do not exercise your intellect regarding their stations, states, and character unless it is by a precise clarification from God, and a consensus of the people who have insight into the proofs which affirm their virtues and ranks. How can you arrive at the reality of what they have from God? If you compare their words and actions with any of the people below them, you will be a bad companion to them; you will have disclaimed their gnosis in ignorance of their being specially selected by God, and you will have dropped below the level of the truths of belief and gnosis. So take care, and take care again.

# CHAPTER 28
# The Recognition
# of the Imams

It is related with a sound chain of authority from Salman al-Farisi, 'I visited the Messenger of God who looked at me and said,

'   "O Salman, God does not send a prophet or messenger unless there are with him twelve chiefs."

'   "O Messenger of God, I know this from the people of the two books."

'   "O Salman, do you know my twelve chiefs, whom God has chosen to be leaders after me?"

'   "God and His Messenger know best."

'   "O Salman, God created me from the quintessence of light, and called me, so I obeyed Him. Then He created `Ali from my light, and called him, and he obeyed. From my light and the light of `Ali He created Fatimah: He called her and she obeyed. From me, `Ali and Fatimah, He created al-Hasan and al-Husayn. He called them and they obeyed Him. God has named us with five of His names: God is *al-Mahmud* (the Praised) and I am Muhammad (worthy of praise); God is *al-`Ali* (the High), and this is `Ali (the one of high rank); God is *al-Fātir* (Creator out of nothing), and this is Fatimah; God is the One with *Ihsān* (beneficence), and this is Hasan; God is *Muhassin* (the Beautiful), and this is Husayn. He created nine Imams from the light of al-Husayn and called them and they obeyed Him, before God created either. Heaven on high, the out-stretched earth, the air, the angels or man. We were lights who glorified Him, listened to Him and obeyed Him."

' "O Messenger of God, may my father and mother be your ransom! What is there for the person who recognizes these men as they should be recognized?"

' "O Salman, whoever recognizes them as they should be recognized, and follows their example, befriends them and is free of their enemies, by God! he is one of us. He will return to where we return, and he will be where we are!"

' "O Messenger of God, is there belief without knowing their names and lineage?"

' "No, Salman."

' "Messenger of God, where will I find them?"

' "You already know al-Husayn; then there will be the master of the worshippers, `Ali ibn Husayn (*Zayn al-`Ābidin*); then his son Muhammad ibn `Ali, the piercer of the knowledge of the early and the later prophets and messengers (*al-Bāqir*); then Ja`far ibn Muhammad, the truthful tongue of God (*al-Sādiq*); then Musa ibn Ja`far, the one who kept his rage silent through patience in God (*al-Kāthim*); then `Ali ibn Musa, pleased with the secret of God (*al-Rida'*); then Muhammad ibn `Ali, the chosen one from the creatures of God (*al-Mukhtār*); then `Ali ibn Muhammad, the guide to God (*al-Hādi*); then al-Hasan, son of `Ali, the silent, trustworthy guardian over the secret of God (*al-`Askari*); then *mīm hā' mim dāl* (Muhammad), called Ibn al-Hasan, the announcer who establishes the right of God.'"

Salman said, 'I wept. Then I continued,

' "O Messenger of God, let my life be deferred until

their time!"

'He said, "O Salman, recite this:

✿  When the promise for the first of the two came,
We sent over you our servants of mighty prowess,
so they went to and fro among the houses, and it
was a promise to be accomplished. Then We gave
you back the turn to prevail against them, and
aided you with wealth and children and made you
a numerous band." (17:5-6)'

"I wept a lot," said Salman, "and my yearning became
intense. I said,
 ' "O Messenger of God, is it a pledge from you?"
 ' "Yes, by the One Who sent me and entrusted me with
the Message; it is a pledge from me and from `Ali, Fatimah,
al-Hasan, al-Husayn, and the nine Imams descended from
the children of al-Husayn, to you and those who are with
us, and those of us who are wronged. Whoever is truly
sincere in his belief, then by God, Salman, let Iblis and his
armies come. Whoever has pure disbelief will be punished
by retaliation, torture and inheritance (i.e. by others rather
than them). Your Lord will not wrong anyone. It is we who
are indicated in this verse:

✿  We desired to bestow a favor upon those who
were deemed weak in the land, and to make them
the leaders, and to make them the heirs, and
to grant them power in the land, and to make
Pharaoh, Haman and their armies see from them
what they feared." (28:5-6)'

Salman said, 'I took leave of the Messenger of God, completely unconcerned as to how Salman would meet death, or how death would meet him.'"

# CHAPTER 29
## Recognition of the Companions

---

Do not forsake certainty for doubt, and what is clear for what is hidden. Do not pass judgment on what you cannot see because of something you are told about it. God despises slander and bad opinion of your believing brothers – what then does He think of boldness in attributing a false statement, false belief or lie to the Companions of the Messenger of God?

As He said:

✿ When you welcomed it with your tongues, and spoke with your mouths that which you had no knowledge of, and you deemed it an easy matter while with Allah it was grievous. (24:15)

As long as you can find a way to speak well and act well of people whether or not they are present, do not do anything else.

God said:

✿ Speak to people good words. (2:83)

Know that God chose companions for His Prophet, honored them with the noblest mark of honor and robed them in the robe of support, victory and the correct keeping of his company in desirable and undesirable situations. He made the tongue of His Prophet speak about their virtues, excellent qualities and marks of honor; so believe in their love, mention their excellence, and beware of the company of people of innovation, for it will make disbelief and clear loss grow in the heart. If the excellence of some of them is not clear to you, then leave them to the Knower of the Unseen, and say, 'O God, I love anyone You and Your Messenger love, and I hate anyone You and Your Messenger hate.' There is no obligation beyond that.

# CHAPTER 30
# The Honor and Sanctity of the Believers

No one respects the honor of the believers except the person who respects the honor and sacred claim of God over the believers. The person who best fulfils this sacred claim with respect to God and His Messenger is he who is the most particular in his respect for the believers' claim to honor. Whoever thinks little of the believers' honor has rent apart the raiment of his belief. The Prophet said, 'Part of esteem for God is to respect those who are near to Allah in belief.' And again, 'Whoever is not merciful to a young person nor respectful to an old person is not one of us. Do not call a Muslim an unbeliever when repentance can make up for it, unless he is someone that God has mentioned in His Book.'

God said:
✧ The hypocrites are in the lowest level of the Fire. (4:145)

Occupy yourself with your business about which you will be questioned.

# CHAPTER 31
## Dutifulness to Parents

Dutifulness to one's parents comes from the bondsman's correct knowledge of God, since there is no act of worship which will bring the person performing it more quickly to the pleasure of God than being dutiful to believing parents for the sake of God. This is because the right of the parents is derived from the right of God, as long as they are both on the path of the faith and the *sunnah*, and do not prevent a child from obeying God for the sake of obedience to them, or move him from certainty to doubt, or from abstinence to the desires of this world, or call him to anything which is in opposition to faith and the *sunnah*. If the situation is like that, then it is an act of obedience to rebel against them, and an act of rebellion to obey them.

God said:

✿ If they contend with you that you should associate with Me what you have no knowledge of, do not obey them. Keep company with them kindly in this world, but follow the way of him who turns to Me, then to Me is your return! (31:15)

As far as companionship is concerned, keep their company and be gentle with them. Endure their hardship just as they endured yours when you were young, and do not withhold from them that which God has made plentiful for you in the way of food and clothes. Do not turn your face away from them nor raise your voice above theirs. To respect them is part of God's command; speak to them in the best possible way and be kind to them. God will not let the reward of those who do good go to waste.

# CHAPTER 32
# Humility

Humility embraces every precious and noble rank and high position. If humility had a language which people understood, it would speak about the realities which are hidden in the outcomes of affairs. Humility is whatever is undertaken for God and in God, and anything other than that is trickery. Whoever is humble to God, God will honor over many of His bondsmen.

The people of humility have recognizable signs. When one of them was asked about humility, he said, 'It means you are humble to the truth and follow it, even if you hear it from a child.' Many types of pride keep one from using, accepting and following knowledge. There are certain verses about this, denouncing the haughty. The people of humility have signs recognized by the angels in heaven and the gnostics on earth.

God said:

&#9788; On the most elevated places there shall be men who know all by their marks. (7:46)

and elsewhere:

&#9788; Whoever from among you turns back from

his faith, then Allah will bring a people whom He loves and they shall love Him, humble towards the believers, mighty against the unbelievers. (5:54)

again:

✿ Surely the most honorable of you with Allah is the one among you with the greatest precaution. (49:13)

and:

✿ So do not claim yourselves to be pure. (53:32)

The root of humility comes from the majesty, awe, and immensity of God. God is not pleased with any act of worship, nor does He accept it unless it comes with humility. No one knows what is the true meaning of humility except those of His bondsmen who are close and connected with His unity.

God said:

✿ The servants of the Merciful are they who walk on earth in humbleness, and when the ignorant address them, they say, Peace. (25:63)

He commanded the mightiest of His creation and the master of its people, Muhammad, to be humble, saying,

✿ Make yourself gentle to the believers. (15:88)

From humility grow submission, humility, fear and modesty; it is only from within humility that these qualities appear. True and perfect nobility is only given to those who are humble in the essence of God.

# CHAPTER 33
## Ignorance

Ignorance is a form whose composition is of this world. When it advances, there is darkness; when it retreats, there is light. The bondsman vacillates with it as shadows vacillate with the sun. Have you not looked at man? Sometimes you find that he is ignorant of his own qualities and praises them, while he recognizes their faults in others and criticizes them. At other times you find that a person knows his own nature and criticizes it, while praising the same in others. He vacillates between protection and disappointment. If he encounters integrity and protection, he is correct. If he encounters lack of assistance and desertion, he errs. The key to ignorance is being satisfied with the knowledge one possesses, and placing all one's trust in it. The key to knowledge is the desire to exchange one level of knowledge for a higher level, together with divine grace and guidance.

The lowest quality of an ignorant man is that he lays claim to knowledge which he does not deserve; his most common characteristic is ignorance of his own ignorance, and the most extreme aspect of his ignorance is to reject knowledge. There is nothing whose affirmation is the reality of its negation other that worldly ignorance and greed. All ignorant people are alike.

# CHAPTER 34
## Eating

A little food is praiseworthy, because it is salutary for the outer and the inner being. Eating is praiseworthy when done out of necessity, as a means and provision, at a time of plenty, or for nourishment. Eating out of necessity is for the pure; eating as a means and provision is a support for the precautious; eating at a time of plenty is for those who trust; and eating for nourishment is for believers.

There is nothing more harmful to the believer's heart than having too much food, for it brings about two things; hardness of heart and arousal of desires. Hunger is a condiment for believers, nourishment for the spirit, food for the heart, and health for the body. The Prophet said, 'The son of Adam fills no worse vessel than his belly.'

David said, 'Leaving a morsel of food that I need is preferable to me than staying up for twenty nights.'

The Messenger of God said, 'The believer eats to fill one stomach, and the hypocrite seven.' And elsewhere, 'Woe to people who are swollen in two places!' When he was asked what they were, he replied, 'The stomach and the genitals.'

Jesus said, 'The heart does not have any worse disease than hardness, and no soul has been more weakened than by lack of hunger. They are two halters of banishment and disappointment.'

# CHAPTER 35
# Evil Whispering

Satan can get control over God's servants only by whispering to them when they have abandoned their remembrance of God, become disdainful, feel complacent when faced with His prohibition, and forget that God sees their secret.

Whispering is what comes from outside the heart by tacit permission of the intellect, and is sustained by man's own nature; once it becomes established in the heart, there is error, misguidance, and disbelief. God called on His bondsmen with His subtle call and told them about the enmity of Iblis:

☼ Shaytan is an enemy to you, so take him as an enemy. (35:6)

Be with him like a man who, standing near the shepherd's dog, has recourse to the dog's master in order to keep the dog away from him. It is the same when Satan comes to whisper to you, to lead you off the true path and make you forget to remember God. Then seek refuge from him with your Lord and his Lord. He will defend the truth against falsehood, and help wronged ones, since He says:

✿ Surely he has no authority over those who believe and who rely on their Lord. (16:99)

Man will only be able to do this if he knows how he comes, and can recognize his methods of whispering, by constant watchfulness, sincerity in the arena of service, awe of the All-Aware, and increased remembrance of Him.

However, anyone who neglects to spend his time in awareness must undoubtedly be the prey of Satan. He should draw a lesson from what Satan does with such a person's self: he leads it to misguidance, deception and haughtiness by duping the person into admiring his own actions, his worship, and his insight. Satan's insolent behavior towards him causes a curse to descend on his knowledge, his gnosis and faculty of reasoning for all eternity; yet he has no power over those who are not negligent. Therefore hold to the firmest rope of God, which means seeking refuge with God, and having a sound need of God at every breath. Do not be deceived when Satan makes your acts of obedience appear beautiful in your eye: if he opens ninety-nine doors of goodness for you, it is only so that he may overcome you by opening the hundredth. So meet him with opposition, block his path and reject his charm.

# CHAPTER 36
## Pride

The concept of pride embraces all those aspects of vanity found in those who are proud of their actions, little knowing what their end will be. Whoever is proud of himself and his actions has strayed off the path of right guidance and has claimed what is not his. Anyone who claims something to which he has no right is a liar, even if he conceals his claim for a long time.

The first thing which happens to the proud man is that he is stripped of his object of pride, so that he will know that he is contemptible and incapable, and will testify against himself; and that will be a firmer proof against him. This was the case with Iblis.

Pride is a plant whose seed is disbelief, whose earth is hypocrisy, and whose water is transgression. Its branches are ignorance, its leaves are misguidance, and its fruit is being cursed to remain in the Fire forever. Whoever chooses pride has sowed disbelief and cultivated hypocrisy. It is inevitable that it must bear its fruit – and he will end up in the Fire.

# CHAPTER 37
# Generosity

Generosity is part of the nature of the prophets, and the buttress of belief. A person cannot be a believer unless he is also generous; he must also have certainty and high aspiration (*himmah*), because generosity is a ray of the light of certainty. Effort is easy for him who knows his objective. The Prophet said, 'The friend of God is but naturally disposed to generosity.'

Generosity is bestowed upon everyone beloved of God who has little of this world. One of the signs of generosity is a lack of concern with the wealth of this world, and with whoever owns it, believing or unbelieving, obedient or rebellious, noble or low. The generous man feeds others while he himself is hungry; he clothes others while he is naked; he gives to others while he refuses to accept the gifts of others. He is favored by that, and does not indebt others by his graciousness. If he were to possess the entire world, he would see himself merely as an alien in it. If he spent it all for God in a single hour, it would not be irksome for him.

The Messenger of God said, 'The generous person is near to God, near to people, near to the Garden and far from the Fire. The miser, however, is far from God, far from people, far from the Garden and near to the Fire.' The only person who can be called generous is the one who expends himself to obey God and for the sake of God, even if it is only by a loaf of bread or a drink of water.

The Prophet also said, 'The person who is generous is generous with what he owns, and through it desires the face of God. As for that person who pretends to be generous and rebels against God, he is the recipient of God's wrath and anger. He is the most miserly of people towards himself, so how must he be with other people, when he follows his own passion and opposes the command of God?'

As God said:

✧    Most certainly they shall carry their own burdens, and other burdens along with their own burdens. (29:13)

The Prophet said, 'The son of Adam cries out, "My property! My property! My wealth! My wealth!" O Wretch! Where were you when there was the Kingdom, and you were not? Is there anything more than what you eat and consume, or what you wear and wear out, or what you give in charity and what you make last?' Either you are shown mercy by it or you are punished for it; therefore use your intelligence, and understand that you should not love the property of others more than your own.

The Commander of the Faithful said, 'What you have already given was destined for those who now own it; what you have held back is for those who will inherit it, and what you have now you have no power over, except to become arrogant by it. How much you strive to seek this world and to make claims! Do you wish to impoverish yourself and enrich others?'

# CHAPTER 38
# Self-reckoning

If there were nothing to make a person turn to self-reckoning (*hisāb*) other than shame at being presented before God and the disgrace of having the veil torn away from his secrets, man would throw himself from the mountaintops and not seek refuge in a building, nor eat, nor drink, nor sleep, except when necessary for preserving his life. This is how a person behaves when he sees the Resurrection, with all its terrors and hardships, with every breath he takes. In his heart he looks at the time when he will stand before the Compelling One, and when he takes account of himself it is as if he were being summoned to that presentation before God, and is being questioned in his death-throes.

God said:

✿ Even though there be the weight of a mustard seed, yet will We bring it and sufficient are We to take account. (21:47)

One of the Imams said, 'Take reckoning from yourselves before you are called to reckoning. Weigh your actions with the scale of your own fear of shame, before they are weighed for you.'

Abu Dharr said, 'The mention of the Garden is death, and so is the mention of the Fire. What a wonder that a person's self lives between two deaths!'

It is related that John the Baptist used to reflect for the entire night on the Garden and the Fire, so that his night was spent in wakefulness and he did not sleep. Then in the morning he would say, 'O God; whither can one flee? Where can one stay? O God, one can only flee to You.'

# CHAPTER 39
## Opening the Prayer

When you face the *qiblah*, you should despair of this world, what it contains of creation and what others are occupied with. Empty your heart of every preoccupation which might distract you from God. See the immensity of God with your innermost being, and remember that you will stand before Him.

For God has said:

☼ There shall every soul become acquainted with what it sent before, and they shall be brought back to Allah, their true Patron. (10:30)

Stand at the foot of fear and hope. When you recite the *takbīr*, you should belittle what is between the high heavens and the moist earth, which are all below His glory, for when God looks into the heart of His bondsman while he is saying the *takbīr*, and sees in his heart something obstructing the truth of his declaring that God is great, He says, 'O liar! Do you try to deceive Me? By My might and My majesty, I will deny you the sweetness of My remembrance, and I will veil you from My nearness and from joy in My intimate communion.'

Know that God does not need your service. He is independent of you, your worship and your supplication. He summons you by His favor to show you mercy, to put you far from His punishment, to spread some of the blessings of His kindness over you, to guide you to the path of His pleasure, and to open to you the door of His forgiveness. If God had created what He created in the universe many times over, forever without end, it would still be the same to God whether they all rejected Him or united with Him. All that He has from the worship of creatures is the display of His generosity and power. Therefore make modesty your cloak and incapacity your shawl. Enter under the throne of the power of God, and you will capture the benefits of His lordship, seeking help in Him and asking for His succor.

# CHAPTER 40
## Bowing in Prayer

The bondsman of God does not truly bow (in *ruku`*) but that God adorns him with the light of His radiance, shades him in the shade of His greatness and clothes him in the garment of His purity. Bowing is first and prostration (*sujud*) is second: there is courtesy in bowing, and in prostration nearness to God. Whoever is not good in the courtesy is not fit for nearness; therefore bow with the *ruku`* of one who is humble to God, abased in his heart and fearful under His power, submitting his limbs to God like one who is fearful and sorrowful for what he might miss of the benefits of those who bow.

It is related that Rabi` ibn Khuthaym used to stay awake all night until dawn, in a single *ruku`*. In the morning he would sigh and say, 'Oh! The sincere have gone ahead, and we are cut off!'

Make your *ruku`* properly by keeping your back straight, coming down from your aspirations in standing to serve Him – which comes only with His help. Let your heart flee from the whisperings, tricks and deceit of Satan. God will elevate His bondsmen according to their humility to Him, and will guide them to the roots of humility, submission and abasement according to how well their innermost being is acquainted with His immensity.

# CHAPTER 41
## Prostration in Prayer

A person who performs true prostration (*sujud*) does not lose God at all, even if it is done only once in his entire life; but the man who deserts his Lord in that state does not prosper. He is like someone who deceives himself, neglecting and forgetting the immediate joy and the ease after this life which God has prepared for those who prostrate themselves.

The person who does well in his prostration is never far from God; while the person who shows ill-courtesy and neglects to honor Him because his heart is attached to something other than God in the state of prostration will never come near to Him. Therefore prostrate yourself with the prostration of someone abased, who knows that he is created from the earth on which people tread, that he is fashioned from sperm which everyone finds impure, and that he was given being when he did not exist.

God made prostration the occasion to draw near to Him in one's heart, innermost being and spirit. Whoever draws near to Him is far from all that is other than Him. Do you not see that in its outward appearance the state of prostrations is not complete except by disappearing from all things and being veiled from all that the eyes see? Thus does God want the inward being to be. If someone's heart is attached to something other than God in prayer, he is near to that thing, and far from the reality of what God desires in His prayer.

For He has said:

☼ Allah has not made for any man two hearts in his breast. (33:4)

In the words of the Messenger of God: 'Almighty God said, "When I look on the heart of a bondsman, I know if he has sincere love and obedience for My sake and seeks My pleasure in it. Then I take charge of him and draw near to him. Whoever is occupied with other-than-Me in his prayer is one of those who mocks himself, and his name is recorded in the register of the losers."'

# CHAPTER 42
# The *Tashahhud*

---

The *tashahhud*[8] is praise of God. Be a slave to Him in your innermost being, fearful and humble to Him in action as you are His bondsman by word and claim. Join the truthfulness of your tongue to the pure truthfulness of your innermost being. He created you a slave and commanded you to worship Him with your heart, your tongue and your limbs. Realize your enslavement to Him by His lordship over you.

Know that the forelocks of creation are all in His hand. Creatures possess neither breath nor sight except by His power and will: they are incapable of bringing forth the least thing in His kingdom, unless it is by His permission and will.

God said:

☼ Your Lord creates and chooses whom he pleases; to choose is not theirs, Glory be to God, and exalted be He above what they associate [with Him]. (28:68)

---

8      Bearing witness (*shahādah*) at the end of each prayer.

Therefore be a slave to God, remembering Him by speech and proclamations, and join the truthfulness of your tongue to the purity of your innermost being, for He created you. He is too mighty and majestic for anyone to have will or volition except by His earlier will and volition. Fulfill the state of enslavement by being content with His wisdom, and by worshipping in order to carry out His commands. He commanded you to send blessings upon His beloved Muhammad, may God bless him and his family and grant them peace. Therefore join your prayer to Muhammad with your prayer to God, obedience to Muhammad to obedience to God, and your witnessing of Muhammad to your witnessing of God. Watch out that you do not miss the blessings of knowledge which are contained in one's respect for his sanctity, with the result that you are denied the benefits of the prayer on him. God commanded him to ask for forgiveness for you, and to intercede for you when you perform what is obligatory in the command and prohibition, and in the *sunnah* and courtesies (*ādāb*) demonstrated to man through the Prophet. You should know the majesty of his rank with God.

# CHAPTER 43
## *Salam*

The meaning of the *taslīm* (greeting of peace) at the end of the prayer means security, that is, anyone who carries out the command of God and the *sunnah* of His Prophet out of humility to Him and showing fear, has security from the tribulations of this world and freedom from the punishment of the next world.

*Al-Salām* (peace) is one of the names of God, which He entrusted to His creation so that they would make use of it in their behavior, trusts, and contracts; in confirming their companies and assemblies; and for the soundness of their social relations. If you want to establish this *salām* in its proper place, and to fulfill its meaning, then fear God; and make your faith, your heart, and your intellect sound. Do not sully them by the injustice of acts of rebellion. Let your guardians be safe from you; do not weary, or bore or alienate them through your bad behavior towards them, nor with your friend, nor with your enemy. If those who are close to someone are not safe from him, then those furthest from him are safest. Anyone who does not establish *salām* on the occasions when it should be established has no peace and no submission; he is a liar in his *salām*, even if he uses it as a form of greeting among people.

Know that man's existence lies between trials and

afflictions in this world. God may test him with blessings, to see his thankfulness, or with hardship, to see if he will show steadfastness and nobility by obeying Him, or disgrace in rebelling against Him, although there is no way to reach His good pleasure and mercy except through His grace. The only means to obey Him is when he grants success: none can intercede with Him except with His permission and mercy.

# CHAPTER 44
## Repentance

Repentance is the rope of God, and the mainstay of His concern for His servants, who must always show repentance, in every state. Each group of bondsmen has its own form of repentance: the repentance of the prophets is for the disquiet caused to their innermost being by any outward source of vexation, while the repentance of the *awliya'* (friends of God) arises from the subtle change of hue in their thoughts. The repentance of the pure lies in their calm abandonment of whatever oppresses them; the repentance of the elite is for being occupied with anything other than God, and the repentance of the common people is for wrong actions. Each of them recognizes and is aware of the cause of his repentance, and his intention therein, but it would take too long to explain all of these here.

As for the repentance of the common man, he washes his inward being with the water of regret, in constant recognition of his wrong action, having regret for what he has done, and fear for what remains of his life. He does not think that his wrong actions are insignificant, for that would lead him to laziness; his continued weeping and regret for what he has missed is in itself an act of worship. He should restrain himself from his worldly appetites, and seek God's help in showing repentance, and to protect him from returning to what he did before. He trains himself in the arena of ignorance and worship. He makes up for obligations missed: he answers others' calls for help, withdraws from bad company, spends his night awake, thirsts during the day, constantly reflecting on his end and seeking help from God, asking Him to make him steady in his states of ease and difficulty, and constant in his trials and afflictions so that he will not fall from the ranks of the repentant. This will purify him of his wrong actions, increase his knowledge, and elevate his rank.

As God has said:

✧ Thus Allah will certainly know those who are truthful, and Allah will certainly know the liars. (29:3)

# CHAPTER 45
# Retreat

Anyone who embarks on a retreat (`uzlah) from the world is fortified by God and protected by His guardianship. What joy there is for the person who has withdrawn with Him, secretly and openly! To do this, he must differentiate between truth and falsehood, love poverty, choose hardship and abstinence, and seize every opportunity for retreat. He must contemplate the outcome of his actions, seeing his incapacity for worship while worshipping as much as possible, abandoning pride, and constantly engaging in remembrance without showing heedlessness, which is the hunting ground of Satan and the beginning of every affliction and the reason for all that is obscure. He should also rid his house of everything he has no immediate need for.

Jesus said, 'Guard your tongue in order to develop your heart, and make your abode be enough for you. Beware of showing off and of having excess provision. Be modest before your Lord and weep for your errors. Flee from people as you flee from the lion and the viper. They were a medicine and now they have become a disease. Then meet God wherever you will.' And Rabi` ibn Khuthaym said, 'If you can manage today to be in a place where you do not know anyone and where none knows you, then do so.'

Retreat brings protection for the limbs, a free heart, a sound livelihood, the destruction of Satan's weapons, the avoidance of every evil and rest for the heart. There is no prophet nor regent (*wasi*) who has not chosen retreat in his lifetime, either at his beginning or at his end.

# CHAPTER 46
## Silence

Silence is the mark of those who are certain of the realities which have already come to be, and about which the Pen has already written. It is the key to every rest in this world and the next: it brings God's pleasure, a lightening of the reckoning and a protection from errors and mistakes. God has made it a veil for the ignorant and an adornment for the man of knowledge.

Through silence, passions can be set aside, and with it come self-discipline, the sweetness of worship, removal of hardhearted-ness, abstinence, virtuousness and resourcefulness. Therefore lock your tongue to speech which is not absolutely necessary, especially when you do not find anyone worth talking to – except, that is, when you are talking specifically about matters to do with God.

Rabi` ibn Khuthaym used to place a parchment before him, upon which he would write down everything he said during the day. In the evening he would call himself to account while he was still alive, seeing what he had said both for and against himself. Then he would say, 'Oh! The silent have indeed been saved!'

One of the Companions of the Messenger of God used to put pebbles in his mouth. When he wanted to say something he knew was both to God, in God and for the sake of God, he would remove them from his mouth. Many of the Companions used to breathe like someone drowning, and speak like someone who was ill.

People's destruction or salvation lies in speech and silence. Good fortune belongs to those who are given knowledge of what is incorrect and correct in speech, and the science of silence and its advantages, for it is one of the qualities of the prophets and one of the distinguishing marks of the select. Whoever knows the value of speech is an export in the company of silence: once a person has been exposed to the subtleties of silence, and has been entrusted with its treasures, then both his speech and silence are worship. No one is privy to this worship of his except the King of all, the All-compelling.

# CHAPTER 47
## Intellect and Passion

The man of intellect submits to what is true and is just in his speech; he shrinks from what is false but opposes it in his speech. He leaves this world behind, but does not leave his faith.

The proof of the man of intellect lies in two things: truthful words and correct actions. The man of intellect does not say something which the intellect rejects, neither does he expose himself to suspicion, nor abandon the help of those who have been tested. Knowledge guides him in his actions; gnosis is his certainty in the paths he treads, and forbearance is his companion at all times. Passion, however, is the enemy of the intellect, the opponent of truth and the companion of falsehood. The strength of passion comes from worldly appetites, and its initial manifestation is caused by doing what is forbidden, neglecting obligations, making light of the *sunnah* and engrossing oneself in amusements.

# CHAPTER 48
## Envy

An envious man harms himself before he harms the person he envies, as was the case with Iblis: by his envy he brought the curse upon himself, whereas to Adam he brought about his election, guidance, elevation to the true contract, and his being chosen. Therefore be envied rather than envious, because the punishment of the envious is always worse than that of the envied; thus is provision apportioned.

So how does envying benefit the envious, and how does envy harm the envied? The root of envy lies in the blindness of the heart, and rejection of God's overflowing favor: they are two wings of disbelief. Through envy the son of Adam falls into endless grief and is utterly destroyed, and there is no way he can save himself. The envious does not really repent, for he continues to dwell upon and believe in his envy; indeed it is such an inherent part of his nature that it manifests itself unopposed and without apparent reason, causing him harm. A person's basic nature does not change, even with treatment.

# CHAPTER 49
# Greed

It is said that Ka`b al-Ahbar was questioned about what is soundest and what is most corrupt in faith. 'The soundest thing is scrupulousness and the most corrupt is greed,' he replied.

Avarice is the wine of Satan, which he gives to his chosen ones with his own hand. Whoever becomes drunk upon it sobers up only in the pain of God's punishment in the proximity of the one who gave him the drink. If there were no other reason for God's wrath with respect to greed except man's preferring this world to faith, that would still be a sufficiently severe chastisement.

God said:

☼ These are they who buy error for the price of right guidance, so their transaction has brought no profit, nor were they guided. (2:16)

The Commander of the Faithful said, 'Be gracious to whoever you wish and you are his prince. Seek help from whoever you like and you are his equal. Be in need of whomever you like and you are his prisoner.' He who is greedy is stripped of his belief without feeling it, for belief prevents the bondsman from being greedy in creation. He also says, 'My friend, the vaults of God are full of marks of honor, and He does not neglect to reward of someone who acts well.'

Whatever a person might possess is tarnished by defects. Belief makes him rely on trust, moderation, forsaking desire, clinging to the obedience of God, and despairing of people. If he does that, then he is keeping close to his belief and he has acted correctly. If he does not, belief parts company with him and leaves him to his bad nature.

# CHAPTER 50
## Corruption

The corruption of the outward being comes from the corruption of the inward. If you put your innermost being in order, God will put your outward being in order; if you fear God inwardly, He will not rend the veil publicly. But he who betrays God inwardly, God will expose in the open.

The greatest corruption is born of prolonged expectation, greed, and pride, as God told us in the story of Qarun[9] when

He said:

✧ Do not seek to make mischief in the land; surely Allah does not love the corruptors. (28:77)

Elsewhere He said:

✧ [As for] that Future Abode, We assign it to those who have no desire to exalt themselves in the earth nor to make mischief; and the good end is for those who have precaution. (28:83)

---

9    Hebrew Korah: cf. Numbers 16:1-35.

These defects come from what Qarun did and believed. The root of corruption lies in loving this world, amassing its wealth; following the self, elevating its appetites, loving praise, agreeing with Satan, and following his footsteps: all of these faults combine with a love of paying God no heed and forgetting His favors.

Therefore you should flee from people, reject this world, interrupt your rest, break with your normal habits, cut off the source of worldly appetites at the root by constantly remembering God and clinging to obedience to Him, and enduring people's aversion, the over-dependence of a comrade, and hostile malice on the part of your family and relatives. If you do that, then the door of God's kindness will be opened to you, since he has good regard for you, as well as forgiveness and mercy. You will have left the company of the heedless and freed your heart from the captivity of Satan. You will come to the door of God in the company of those who come to Him, and you will travel a path on which you may hope to be permitted to come to the Noble, the Magnanimous, the Generous, the Merciful.

# CHAPTER 51
# Well-being

Seek well-being (*salamah*) from God wherever you are in every state you may be in, for your faith, your heart, and the ultimate outcome of your affairs. He who seeks it does not always find it. How then, is it that there are some who expose themselves to affliction, travel the opposite path to well-being and oppose its principles, seeing safety as destruction and destruction as safety?

Well-being has been taken away from people in every age, especially this one; yet it can be rediscovered through enduring antipathy and even injury from other people, through patience in the face of disaster, making light of death, fleeing from whatever is reprehensible and being content with a minimum of material possessions. If you are not like that, then you must go into retreat. If you cannot do that then be silent, although silence is not the same as retreat. If you cannot be silent, then speak what will help you and not harm you; but that is not the same thing as silence. If you cannot find any way to do that, then move about by journeying from land to land,[10] casting your self

---

10    According to a tradition the Prophet said, 'A time will come ... when the man of faith will not be safe until he flees from one lofty spring to another.'

(*nafs*) into the uncharted territories with a pure intention, humble heart, and steadfast body.

God said:

✧ Surely, [as for] those whom the angels cause to die while they are unjust to their souls, they shall say, "In what state were you?" They shall say, "We were oppressed in the land." They shall say, "Was not Allah's earth spacious so that you could have migrated therein?" (4:97)

Take whatever belongs to the rightly acting bondsmen of God. Do not struggle with obscure matters, nor contend with contradictions. If anyone tells you, 'I', say 'you'. Do not claim knowledge in anything, even if you are an expert in it. Uncover your secret only to one who is nobler in the faith than you, and thus you will find nobility. If you do this you will obtain well-being, and you will remain with Almighty without any connection to anything else.

# CHAPTER 52
# Worship

Persevere in performing the customs and obligations in worship (`ibādah`), for they are the source: whoever obtains them and performs them properly has obtained everything. The best form of worship is that which comes nearest to security – this is the one most free of harm and the most consistent, be it ever so small. If you have performed your obligatory and supererogatory prayers, then you are a true worshipper.

Beware of treading on the carpet of a king unless you do so with abasement, acknowledgement of need, fear, and respect. Make your movements free of showing off and your secret free of hardness.

The Prophet said, 'The person who prays is conversing with his Lord.' So be embarrassed before the One Who is Cognizant of your secret, Who knows your conversation and what your conscience conceals. Beware He will see you doing what He wants you to do, and performing that to which He has summoned you. Those who have gone before us occupied themselves from the moment they completed one obligatory prayer to the moment they started another, so that they could perform both prayers sincerely and correctly. It seems that in our times it has become a virtue to leave the obligatory aside, which is like having a body without a soul.

`Ali ibn al-Husayn said, 'I wonder at a person who seeks something extra while he abandons an obligation; he only does so because he lacks recognition of the matter and respect for it. He does not see God's will in preparing people to obey His command and choosing that for them.'

# CHAPTER 53
## Reflection

Reflect on what has passed of this world. Has any of it remained for anyone? Has anyone remained in it, be he noble or lowly, rich or poor, friend or enemy? Similarly, what has not yet happened of it resembles more closely that which has passed of it, than water resembles water.

The Messenger of God said:

✪ 'Death is enough of a warner;

✪ the intellect is enough of a guide;

✪ precaution is enough of a provision;

✪ worship is enough of an occupation;

✪ God is sufficient as an intimate friend;

✪ the Qur'an is enough of a clarification.'

And elsewhere, 'Only affliction and trial remain of this world. If a person is saved, it is only by sincerely seeking refuge,' And Noah said, 'I found this world to be like a house with two doors. I entered through one of them and went out through the other.' Such is the state of the one who was saved by God: so what is the state of one who feels at ease in this world, relies on it, wastes his life by cultivating it, and is full of worldly demands?

Reflection is the mirror of good deeds and the expiation of bad deeds. It is the light of the heart, and guarantees ease to other people and success in obtaining betterment for the Next Abode; it allows one to foresee the outcome of one's actions, and causes an increase in knowledge. Worship of God is unparalleled when accompanied by this quality. The Messenger of God said, 'To reflect for an hour is better than worshipping for a year.' The station of reflection is only obtained by him whom God has singled out for the light of gnosis (*ma`rifah*) and *tawhīd*.

# CHAPTER 54
# Rest

The believer only acquires true rest when he meets God, although rest may also be obtained by these four things: silence, by which you recognize the state of your heart and your self in your relations with your Creator; retreat, by which you are rescued from the evils of the age, outwardly and inwardly; hunger, which kills fleshly appetites and temptation; and wakefulness, which illuminates your heart, purifies your nature and cleanses your spirit.

The Prophet said, 'If a man finds himself in the morning tranquil in his heart, healthy in body and with food for the day, it is as if all of this world had been chosen for him'; and Wahb ibn Munabbih quoted the first and latter prophets as saying, 'O contentment, honor and riches are to be found with you. Whoever wins, wins through you!'

Abu al-Darda' said, 'What God has allotted to me will not pass me by, even if it were on the wing of a breeze'; and Abu Dharr said, 'The secret of a man who does not trust his Lord is always exposed, even if it is imprisoned in solid rock.' No one is in a greater state of loss, is viler or lower than the person who does not believe what his Lord has guaranteed for him and allotted him before He created him. In spite of that, this person relies on his own strength, management, effort, and striving, and goes beyond the limits of his Lord by his seeking ways and means which God has caused him to have no need of.

# CHAPTER 55
# Avarice

Do not covet anything avariciously; for if you ignore it, it will come to you anyway, if it is destined to be yours. Then you would find ease in your heart with God, praise for leaving it; but you will be blamed for your haste in seeking it, for not trusting Him, and for not being content with the decree. God created this world the same as a shadow: when you chase it, it tires you out and you can never catch up with it. If you leave it alone, it follows you inexorably, and gives you no cause for fatigue.

The Prophet said, 'A covetous man is bereft; yet in spite of his deprivation, he is blamed wherever he is.' For how could he be other than bereft when he flees from the covenant of God, and opposes

His words:

✿ Allah is He Who created you, then gave you sustenance, then He causes you to die, then brings you life. (30:40)

The covetous person is in the midst of seven difficult evils: thinking, which harms his body but brings it no help; anxiety, which has no end; weariness, from which he will find rest only in death, although he has the greatest weariness when at rest; fear, which only makes him fall into what he fears; sorrow, which makes his livelihood disturbed without any benefit to him; reckoning, which will not save him from the punishment of God unless He pardons him, and punishment, from which there is neither flight nor escape.

The one who trusts in God spends morning and evening m His protection and well-being. God has hastened for him what suffices him, and prepared for him things which only God knows. Avarice is what flows out from God's anger. When the slave is not bereft of certainty, he is not covetous. Certainty is the earth of Islam and the heaven of *imān*.[11]

---

11     Faith; Belief, but with knowledge.

# CHAPTER 56
# Clarification

The intimate conversation of the gnostics possesses three roots: fear, hope and love. Fear is the branch of knowledge; hope is the branch of certainty, and love is the branch of gnosis (*ma`rifah*). The proof of fear is flight; the proof of hope is quest, and the proof of love is preferring the Beloved over all others.

When knowledge is confirmed in truthfulness, he fears. When fear is genuine, he flees. When he flees, he is saved. When he sees the light of certainty in the heart, he sees overflowing favor. When the vision of overflowing favor is firm, there is hope. When he feels the sweetness of belief in hope, he seeks. When he has success in the quest, he finds. When the light of gnosis is manifested in his heart, the breeze of love stirs, he settles in the shadow of the Beloved, prefers the Beloved over all others, follows His commands and avoids His prohibitions, and chooses them over everything else. When he perseveres towards intimacy with the Beloved while carrying out His commands and avoiding His prohibitions, he has reached the spirit of intimate communion and nearness.

These three roots are like the sanctuary, the mosque, and the Ka`bah: whoever enters the Sacred Precinct is safe from people. If a person enters the mosque, his senses are safe from being used in disobedience, and if a person enters the Ka'bah, his heart is safe from being occupied with anything other than the remembrance of God.

Take heed, O believer! If you are in a state in which you are content to meet death, then thank God for His grace and protection. If it is other than that, then move from it with sound resolution, and have regret for that part of your life which passed in heedlessness. Seek God's help in purifying your outward nature of wrong actions and cleanse your inward being from faults. Cut the shackles of heedlessness from your heart, and extinguish the fire of desires in your soul.

# CHAPTER 57
## Judgments

The heart may be described as belonging to one of four types: uplifted, open, low, or stopped. The *raf* (uplifting) of the heart lies in remembrance of God; the *fath* (opening) of the heart lies in the pleasure of God; the *khafd* (lowering) of the heart lies in occupation with anything other than God, and the *waqf* (stopping) of the heart lies in paying no heed to anything other than God.[12]

Do you not see that when a servant remembers God with sincere respect, every veil that was between him and God is removed? If the heart obeys the source of God's decree and is content with that, then how do happiness, joy and worldly rest open up to him? When the heart is occupied with some of the matters of this world and its means, how, then, can it find what God has mentioned? Then the heart becomes reduced and dark like an empty, ruined house which has neither prosperity nor occupant. When a person is distracted from remembering God, then you see that he is 'stopped' from advancing, and veiled.

---

12     These are all Arabic indications of nominal vowel-endings and declension. *Raf* ('raising') denotes the nominative -*u* sound; *fath* ('opening') denotes the accusative –*a* sound; *khafd* ('lowering') denotes the genitive -*i* sound; and *waaf* ('stopping') denotes the absence of a vowel.

He has become obdurate and dark since leaving the light which issues from the servant's veneration of his Lord.

The sign of *raf* lies in agreement in every respect, lack of opposition, and constant yearning; the sign of *fath* lies in trustful dependence on God, truthfulness and certainty; the sign of *khafd* lies in pride, showing off, and greed; and the sign of *waqf* lies in the departure of the sweetness of obedience, lack of the bitterness of rebellion, and of confusion in the knowledge of what is permitted and what is forbidden.

# CHAPTER 58
## *Siwak*

The Messenger of God said, 'Using the *siwāk*[13] purifies the mouth and is pleasing to the Lord,' and he made it one of the confirmed practices. It has benefits for both the outward and the inward being which even men of intelligence cannot count.

As you remove the stains caused by food and drink from your teeth with the *siwāk*, so remove the impurity of your wrong actions by humble entreaty, humility, night prayers, and asking for forgiveness before dawn. Purify your outer being from impurities, and your inner being from the turbidity of acts of opposition and committing anything prohibited, all the while acting sincerely for God. The Prophet made its use an example for people for alertness and attention, in that the *siwāk* is a clean, soft plant and the twig of a blessed tree. The teeth are what God created in the mouth as a tool for eating, an implement for chewing, a reason for enjoying food and for keeping the intestines in order. The teeth are pure jewels, which become dirty because they are present when food is chewed, leading to a deterioration in the way the mouth smells, and decay in

---

13      A small stick used for cleaning the teeth.

the gums. When the intelligent believer cleans with the soft plant and wipes it on these pure jewels, he removes the decay and adulteration from them and they then revert to their original state.

Similarly God created the heart pure and clean, and made its food remembrance, reflection, awe and respect. When the pure heart turns grey by being fed on heedlessness and vexation, it is polished by the burnish of repentance and cleaned by the water of regret, so that it reverts to its primal state and its basic essence.

As God said:

✿ Surely Allah loves those who turn [in repentance] to Him, and He loves those who purify themselves. (2:222)

In recommending the use of the *siwāk* the Prophet was advocating that it be used on the teeth themselves; but he also implied the meaning and example we have referred to above, that for anyone who empties his faculty of reflection for the purpose of drawing inward lessons from the outward examples – with respect to both the principle and roots of faith – God will open the springs of wisdom, and will give him still more of His overflowing favor, for God does not neglect the reward of those who act well.

# CHAPTER 59
# Using the Lavatory

The lavatory is called in Arabic 'the place of rest', because there people may find rest from the burden of impurities and empty themselves of grossness and filth. There the believer may reflect on how he is cleansing himself from the food and perishable matter of this world, and how his own death will come in like manner: therefore he should find ease in avoiding the world, leaving it aside and freeing himself and his heart from its distractions. He should be averse to taking and gathering this world just as he loathes impurity, the lavatory and filth, reflecting on how something good in one state becomes so base in another. He knows that holding onto contentment and precaution will bring him ease in the two abodes.

Thus ease comes from considering this world to be insignificant, giving up one's enjoyment of it, and removing the impurity of what is forbidden or doubtful. A person closes the door of pride on himself once he recognizes this; he flees from wrong actions and opens the door of humility, regret, and modesty. He strives to carry out God's commands and to avoid His prohibitions, seeking a good end and excellent proximity to God. He locks himself in the prison of fear, steadfastness, and the restraint of his appetites until he reaches the safety of God in the world to come, and tastes the food of His good pleasure. If he intends that, everything else means nothing to him.

# CHAPTER 60
## Purification

If you seek purification and ablution (*wudu'*), then go to water as you would go to the mercy of God, for He has made water the key to being near to Him in intimate conversation, and a guide to the domain of His service. Just as the mercy of God purifies the wrong actions of His bondsmen, so are outward impurities cleansed only by water.

As God said:

✧ It is He Who sends the winds as good news before His mercy; and We send down pure water out of heaven! (25:48)

and elsewhere:

✧ We have made of water everything living. Will they not then believe? (21:30)

As He gives life to every blessing in this world from water, so by His mercy and overflowing favor He gives life to the heart and to acts of obedience, and to reflection in the purity of water, its fineness, its cleanness, its blessing and the subtleness of how it mixes with everything; through water He also gives life to the heart, when you purify those limbs which you have been commanded by God to purify, and which you use to worship in your obligatory and customary prayers.

From each limb come many benefits. When you treat the limbs with respect, then their benefits will soon spring up for you. Deal with God's creation like water which mixes with things and gives everything its due, while not changing itself in essence. This is expressed by the words of the Messenger of God, 'The sincere believer is like water.' Let your purity with God in all your obedience be like the purity of water when He sent it down out of heaven and called it pure. Purify your heart with precaution and certainty when you purify your limbs with water.

# CHAPTER 61
## Entering the Mosque

---

When you reach the door of the mosque, know that you have come to the door of a mighty King. Only the purified tread on His carpet and only the true are allowed to sit with Him. So be alert in your approach of the court of the awesome King, for you are in great danger if you are heedless. Know that He can do whatever He wishes in justice and overflowing favor with you and by you. If He inclines to you with His mercy and overflowing favor, He has accepted a small amount of your obedience and has given you a great reward for it. If He demands His due of truthfulness and sincerity by His justice towards you, He has veiled you and rejected your obedience, even if you have had obedience in abundance. He does what He wills. Acknowledge your incapacity, inadequacy, fragility, and poverty before Him, for you have turned yourself to worshipping Him and being close to Him. Turn to Him, and know that neither the secret nor the revealed part of any creature is hidden from Him. Be like the poorest of His servants before Him: strip your heart of every occupation which might veil you from your Lord, for He only accepts the purest and most sincere. Look to see in which register your name will be written.

If you taste the sweetness of His intimate conversation

and the pleasure of His addressing you, and drink the cup of His mercy, and those favors he has bestowed on you and those of your requests which He has accepted, then you have served Him properly, and may therefore enter the sphere of His permission arid security. If not, then stand as one whose power and ability have been cut off, and whose term has come to an end. If Almighty God knows that in your heart you are sincerely seeking refuge with Him, He will regard you with compassion, mercy and kindness. He will cause you to succeed in that which He loves and which is pleasing to Him, for He is generous. He loves noble generosity and the worship of those who need Him, and who are burning up at His door seeking His good pleasure.

God said:

✷ Who answers the distressed one when he calls upon Him, and removes the evil? (27:62)

# CHAPTER 62
## Supplication

Observe the courtesy of supplication. Consider the One on whom you call, how you call on Him and why you call; affirm the immensity and magnificence of God. Look with your heart at how He knows what is in your conscience, how He sees your secret being and whatever has occurred and will occur in it, both true and false. Learn the paths to your salvation and destruction, so that you do not call upon God for something which perhaps contains your destruction, but which you suppose to contain your salvation.

God said:

✿ Man prays for evil as he ought to pray for good, and man is ever hasty. (17:11)

Reflect about what you ask for and why you are asking: supplication should be a total response to the Truth on your part, and a melting of the heart in contemplation of its Lord. It is to abandon all choices and to surrender all matters, both outward and inward, to God. If the preconditions of the supplication are not met, then do not look for fulfillment, for He knows what is secret and what is hidden; you might ask Him for something when He knows that you conceal the opposite of it.

One of the companions said to the others, 'You are waiting for rain, and I am waiting for stones.' Know that if God had not commanded us to call on Him, He would nevertheless have favored us with an answer immediately after we finished the prayer – how, then, is His favor, given the fact that He has guaranteed that answer to whoever fulfils the conditions of the prayer?

The Messenger of God was asked about the most powerful name of God: he said, 'Every name of God is most powerful.' Free your heart from all that is other-than-Him, and call on Him by whatever name you like. In reality God does not have one name rather than another: He is God, the One, the Almighty.

The Prophet said, 'God does not answer the supplication of a heedless heart.' When one of you wants His Lord to give to him whatever he asks of Him, he should renounce all people, putting his hope in God alone. When God sees that in his heart, He will give him whatever he asks.

When you have established the preconditions of supplication which I have mentioned, and have become sincere in your innermost being for His sake, then rejoice in the good news that one of three things will happen: either He will hasten to give you what you have asked for, or He will store up something better for you, or He will avert from you an affliction which would have destroyed you had He sent it. The Prophet reported that God said, 'If anyone is distracted from asking Me by his own remembrance of Me, I will give him better than what I give to those who ask.'

I called on God once and He answered me. I forgot the need because of the fact that when He answers a supplication, His bestowal is far greater and more sublime than what the bondsman desires from Him, even if it be the Garden and its eternal blessings. This is understood only by lovers who act, gnostics, the elite and the select of God.

# CHAPTER 63
## Fasting

The Prophet said, 'Fasting is a protection from the calamities of this world, and a veil from punishment of the next.' When you fast, intend thereby to restrain your self from fleshly appetites and to cut off those worldly desires arising from the ideas of Satan and his kind. Put yourself in the position of a sick person who desires neither food nor drink; expect recovery at any moment from the sickness of wrong actions. Purify your inner being of every lie, turbidity, heedlessness and darkness which might cut you off from the meaning of being sincere for the sake of God.

Somebody said to one of the Companions, 'You are already weak; fasting will weaken you further.' 'I am preparing that fast for the evil of a long day,' he said. 'Patience in obeying God is easier than patience in His punishment.' And the Messenger of God once quoted God's words, 'Fasting is done for Me, and I am its reward.'

Fasting kills the desire of the self and the appetite of greed, and from it comes purity of the heart, purification of the limbs, cultivation of the inner and the outer being, thankfulness for blessings, charity to the poor, increase of humble supplication, humility, weeping and most of the ways of seeking refuge in God; and it is the reason for the breaking of aspiration, the lightening of evil things, and the redoubling of good deeds. It contains benefits which cannot be counted. It is enough that we mention some of them to the person who understands and is given success in making use of fasting, if God wills.

# CHAPTER 64
## Abstinence

Abstinence is the key to the door of the next world and freedom from the Fire. It consists of leaving everything which could distract you from God without regret, nor feeling proud about leaving it, nor waiting for relief from your renunciation, nor seeking any praise for it. Indeed abstinence means a person considering such things to be of no avail to him: he deems their passing him by as a relief and comfort for him and their presence as a misfortune for him; thus he always flees from misfortune and clings to what brings him ease and relief. The man of abstinence is the one who chooses the next world. He chooses abasement over might and this world, striving over rest, hunger over being full, the well-being of what is to come later over immediate trials and remembrance over heedlessness. His self is in this world and his heart is in the next world.

The Messenger of God said, 'Love of this world is the fount of every error;' and elsewhere, 'This world is a corpse; whoever seeks it is like a dog.' Do you not see how it loves what God hates? What error is a greater crime than this?

One of the Prophet's family said, 'If all of this world were a morsel in a child's mouth, we would have mercy on him. What then is the state of someone who throws the limits set by God behind his back, seeking and desiring this world? If the dwelling place of this world had been any good, it would not have shown you mercy, nor answered you, and would have bidden you farewell in departure.'

The Messenger of God said, 'When Almighty God created this world, He commanded it to obey Him and it obeyed its Lord. He told it, "Oppose the one who seeks you and give success to the one who opposes you."' It acts according to what God charged it to do, and what He impressed upon its nature.

# CHAPTER 65
# A Description of this World

This world is like a body whose head is pride, whose eyes are avarice, whose ears are greed, whose tongue is dissimulation, whose hand is desire, whose legs are vanity, whose heart is heedlessness, whose being is annihilation, and whose product is extinction.

It brings pride to whoever loves it, avarice to whoever prefers it, greed to whoever seeks it, and cloaks with hypocrisy whoever praises it. It gives vanity power over whoever desires it; it leads to heedlessness in the person who relies on it. It seduces whoever admires its goods, but those goods do not last for him. It returns the person who gathers it and is miserly with it to its own abode, which is the Fire.

# CHAPTER 66
# Reluctance to Act

A person who feels reluctant to act falls short of what is correct, even if he does right; while a person who acts voluntarily is correct, even if he errs. The reluctant one obtains only contempt in the end, and weariness, toil and misery while he is carrying out the action. The outer being of a reluctant person is showing off, and his inner being is hypocrisy: they are the wings with which he flies. The reluctant person never has any of the qualities of the righteous nor any of the marks of the believers, wherever he is.

As God said to His Prophet:

✿ Say, I do not ask you for any reward for it; nor am I of those who affect [i.e. act with reluctance]. (38:86)

The Prophet said, 'We, the company of prophets, the fearfully aware, the trusty, we disavow the reluctant.' So, fear God and do away with reluctance, and it will mark you with the sign of belief. Do not be occupied with something whose garment is affliction, with food which in the end is emptiness, with an abode whose end is ruin, with wealth whose end is to be inherited by others, with comrades whom in the end one must take leave of, with glory which in the end is abasement, with loyalty which in the end is abandonment, or with a life whose end is grief.

# CHAPTER 67
## Delusion

A person who is deluded is wretched in this world, and is duped in the next world because he has sold what is better for what is baser. Do not admire yourself. Sometimes you may be deceived by your property and your bodily health into supposing that you will last forever. Sometimes you are deceived by your long life, your children and your friends into thinking that you will be saved by them. Sometimes you are deceived by your beauty and the circumstances of your birth, which bring you your hopes and desires so easily that you think that you are truthful and successful in achieving your goal. Sometimes you are deceived by the regret you show people for your shortcoming in worship, but God knows the opposite of that is in your heart. Sometimes you make yourself worship in a spirit of reluctance; but God desires sincerity. Sometimes you imagine that you are calling on God when you are calling on another. Sometimes you imagine that you are giving good counsel to people, while your real desire is that they bow to you. Sometimes you blame yourself when you are really praising yourself.

Know that you will only emerge from the darkness of delusion and desire by sincerely turning in repentance to Almighty God, and to whatever you know about Him, and to recognize the faults in your self which are not consistent with your intellect and knowledge, and which the faith, the law and the customary practices of the Prophet and the Imams of guidance do not tolerate.

If you are content with your present condition, there is no one more wretched than you in knowledge and action, nor anyone with a more wasted life. You will inherit grief on the Day of Resurrection.

# CHAPTER 68
# A Description of the Hypocrite

The hypocrite is content to be far from the mercy of God, because his outward actions appear to be in line with Islamic laws; and yet he is heedless and ineffective, mocking and transgressing its truthfulness in his heart.

The mark of hypocrisy is disregard for lies, treachery, insolence, false claims, insincerity, foolishness, error and lack of modesty, making little of acts of disobedience, desiring believers to lose faith, and making light of misfortunes in the faith, pride, praise, praise of love, love of praise, envy, preferring this world to the next and evil to good, inciting slander, love of amusement, dealing with prevaricators, helping aggressive people avoiding good deeds, disparaging those who do good, considering good the evil done by the hypocrite and recognizing as odious whatever good another person does; and many other things like that.

God has described the hypocrites in more than one place.

He said:

☼ And among people is he who serves Allah [standing] on the verge. So that if good befalls him he is satisfied therewith, but if a trial afflicts him he turns back headlong; he loses this world as well as the next; that is a manifest loss. (22:11)

In describing them, God said:

☼ There are some people who say, "We believe in Allah and the Last Day", but they are not at all believers. They desire to deceive Allah and those who believe, but they deceive only themselves while they do not perceive. There is a disease in their hearts, so Allah added to their disease. (2:8-10)

The Prophet said, 'The hypocrite is he who, having made a promise, breaks it; when he acts, he does evil; when he speaks, he lies; when he is trusted, he betrays; when he is given provision, he is reckless; when it is withheld, he makes much of his life.'

He also said, 'A person whose innermost being contradicts his public face is a hypocrite whoever he is, wherever he is, in whatever time he lives, and whatever rank he has.'

# CHAPTER 69
# Proper Social Transaction

$B$ehaving correctly with Almighty God's creation without disobedience to Him comes from God's increased favor to His bondsmen. Whoever is humble to God in his heart behaves well openly.

Keep company with people for the sake of God, not for your portion of something which belongs to this world or to seek position or for showing off or to increase your own reputation. Do not cross the limits of the Law for the sake of eminence and fame: they will not profit you at all, and you will miss the next world without gaining any benefit.

# CHAPTER 70
## Taking and Giving

A person who prefers taking to giving is deluded, because in his heedlessness he thinks that what is now is better than what is to come. It behooves the believer, when he takes something, that he should take it rightfully. If he gives, it should be for a right purpose, in a right way, and from his rightful possessions. How many a taker gives up his faith, but he is not aware of that! How many a giver brings down on himself the wrath of God! The matter is not just a question of taking and giving, however; rather he is saved who fears God when taking and giving, and who holds tight to the rope of righteousness.

In this regard people are of two types: the elite and the common. The elite considers with painstaking caution and does not take until he is certain that it is permissible. If it is unclear to him, he will only take when it is absolutely necessary. The common man considers only the outward form: he takes whatever he does not find to be stolen or extorted, and says, 'There is no harm in this: it is permissible for me.' Here the matter is clear, and he takes it by the judgment of Almighty God and spends it in His pleasure.

# CHAPTER 71
# Brotherhood

Three things are rare in every age: brotherhood in God; a devout, affectionate wife who helps you in God's faith; and a rightly guided son. Whoever finds these three things has obtained the good of both abodes and the fullest portion of this world and the next. Beware of taking someone as a brother when you are moved by greed, fear, inclination, money, food or drink. Seek the fraternity of the God-fearing, even to the ends of the earth, and even if you spend your entire life seeking them. God has not left anyone better than them after the Prophets on the face of the earth, nor has He given a bondsman any blessing like that of success in finding their company.

God has said:

✧ The friends shall on that day be enemies to one another except those who guard [against evil]. (43:67)

I believe that anyone who looks for a friend without fault in these times will remain without a friend. Do you not see that the first mark of honor which God bestowed on His Prophets when their call to faith became known was a trusty friend or helper. Similarly, the most sublime gift which God bestowed on His friends, supporters (*awliya'*), pure friends and trustees was the company of His prophets. This is proof that, after knowledge of God, there is no blessing in either abode which is more sublime, more excellent or more pure than company in God and brotherhood for His sake.

# CHAPTER 72
## Consultation

Take counsel in the matters faith demands of you with one who has the following five qualities: intellect, knowledge, experience, good counsel, and precaution. If you find these five things in a person, then make use of them, be resolute and rely on God. This will lead you to what is correct.

As for matters of this world which do not pertain to faith, make decisions about them and then do not think about them further. If you do this, you will obtain the blessings of livelihood and the sweetness of obedience.

Knowledge is obtained through consultation. The man of intellect is he who derives new knowledge from consultation, and that guides him to obtain his goal. Consulting a proper counselor is like reflecting upon the creation of the heavens and the earth and the destruction of both, since the more intense a person's reflection upon these two things, the deeper he penetrates into the seas of the light of gnosis and the more he increases his understanding and certainty.

Do not take counsel from someone when your intellect does not give him any credence, even if he is famous for his discernment and scrupulousness. When you take counsel from someone your heart trusts, do not disagree with what he advises even if it is contrary to what you want. Surely the self combines both acceptance of the truth with what is opposed to it – that is, on receiving other truths which are clearer to him.

God has said:

☼ Take counsel with them in the affair. (3:159)

and again:

☼ Their rule is to take counsel among themselves. (42:38)

that is, they consult each other about it.

# CHAPTER 73
## Forbearance

Forbearance is a lamp of God which leads the holder to His excellence; a person cannot be forbearing unless he is aided by the lights of gnosis and *tawhīd*. Forbearance has five facets: when a man is exalted, but is then humbled; when he is truthful, he is accused of being a liar; when he calls people to the truth, he is scorned; when he is injured without having done any crime; and when he demands his rights and they oppose him.

When you have given each of these its due, you have achieved the goal. When you have countered the half-wit by turning away from him and not answering him, people will come to your aid, for he who wages war with a fool is like a man who puts wood on the fire.

The Prophet said, 'The believer is like the earth: people obtain benefits from it while they are on it.' Whoever cannot endure people's harsh rudeness will not reach God's good pleasure, because His pleasure is closely linked with people's antipathy. It is related that a man said to Ahnaf ibn Qays, 'You are causing me to worry.' He replied, 'I will forbear with you.'

The Messenger of God said, 'I was sent as a center of forbearance, a mine of knowledge, and a home for patience.' He spoke the truth when he said, 'True forbearance is when you pardon a person who acts badly with you and opposes you, while you have the power to take revenge on him.' It is as the supplication says: 'My God, You are too vast in favor and forbearance to punish me for my action and abase me for my mistake.'

# CHAPTER 74
## Following Another's Example

Following the example of another is nothing more than what has been bestowed upon the spirit at its origin, when the light of time was mixed with that of eternity. Following a model, however, does not consist of adopting the marks of outward actions and claiming descent from the *awliya'* of the faith from among the wise and the Imams.

As God said:

✧ The day when We will call every people by their Imam. (17:71)

that is, whoever follows someone with effacement is pure. And elsewhere:

✧ So when the trumpet is blown, there will be no ties of relationship between them on that day, nor shall they ask of each other. (23:101)

The Commander of the Faithful said, 'Souls are a drafted army. Those who know each other are intimate, and those who do not know each other differ from each other.' Muhammad ibn al-Hanafiyah was asked who had taught him good manners, and he replied, 'My Lord taught me manners in myself. Whatever I find to be good in people of intelligence and insight I follow and use; whatever I find ugly in the ignorant I avoid and forsake forever. That has brought me to the path of knowledge. There is no sounder way for the astute believer than to follow the example of others, because it is the clearest path and soundest goal.' And God said to Muhammad, the greatest of His creation:

✿ These are they whom Allah guided, therefore follow their guidance. (6:90)

Elsewhere He said:

✿ Then We revealed to you: Follow the faith of Abraham, the upright one. (16:123)

If the faith of God had had a path straighter than following a model, He would have recommended it to His prophets and His supporters.

The Prophet said, 'There is a light in the heart which is illuminated only by following the truth and intending towards the right path. It is a part of the light of the prophets which has been entrusted in the hearts of the believers.'

# CHAPTER 75
## Pardon

Pardoning someone when you have the power to punish is one of the customary practices of the messengers and the secrets of the God-fearing. Pardon is when you do not charge your companion for what he has done wrong outwardly, when you forget the cause by which there was inward affliction, and when you extend great charity in your choice despite having power over him. No one could find a way to that pardon except by the one whom God has pardoned and forgiven for the sins which he has committed and the deeds he has put off, and who has been adorned with His mark of honor and clothed in the light of His radiance. This is because pardon and forgiveness are two of the attributes of Almighty God which He entrusted in the secrets of His pure friends, so that they adopt the manners of their Creator and Maker with creation. This is why

He said:

☼ They should pardon and turn away. Do you not love that Allah should forgive you? And Allah is forgiving, merciful. (24:22)

If you do not pardon another mortal like yourself, how can you hope for the pardon of the Compelling King?

The Prophet said that his Lord commanded him to have these qualities, saying, 'Unite with whoever breaks with you, and pardon whoever wrongs you; give to whoever deprives you, and be good to whoever is bad to you.' He commanded us to follow him when God said:

✿ Whatever the Messenger gives you, accept it, and from whatever he forbids you, keep back. (59:7)

Pardon is a secret of God in the heart of His select. Whoever is gladdened by it has made Him happy. The Messenger of God said, 'Is any of you capable of being like Abu Damdam?' 'O Messenger of God,' they said, 'Who is Abu Damdam?' The Prophet replied, 'One of your ancestors who, when he woke up in the morning would say, "O God, I have forgiven the shattering of my honor by the common people."'

# CHAPTER 76
## Exhortation

The best form of exhortation is when the words used do not go beyond the limits of truth, and the actions performed do not go beyond the limits of sincerity. The warner and the warned are like someone awake and someone asleep: whoever awakes from the slumber of his heedlessness, opposition and rebellion does good to awaken others from that sleep.

Anyone who travels in the deserts of transgression and engrosses himself in the wilds of misguidance, abandons his modesty because of his love for reputation, showing off and fame, wasting his time with those who wear the garments of the righteous, his outward appearance divulging the substance, of what is inside of him. In reality he is devoid of any substance and his inner destitution is flooded with love of praise and enveloped in the darkness of greed. How seduced he is by his passion! How he leads people astray with his words!

As God has said:

✿ Evil certainly is the guardian and evil certainly is the associate. (22:13)

But whoever God has protected by the light of *tawhīd*, support, and excellent success, his heart is cleansed of impurity. He does not separate himself from gnosis and precaution; he listens to the words of the misguided while he ignores the speaker himself, whoever he is. The wise have said, 'Take wisdom, even if it comes from the mouths of madmen.' In the words of Jesus, 'Sit with anyone who reminds you of God when you see him and meet him, aside from when he talks. Do not sit with someone when your outer being accepts him but your inner being rejects him.' That is someone who lays claim to what he does not have; if you are sincere, then they will yield to you. When you find someone with these three qualities, then seize the opportunity to see him, meet with him, and sit with him, even if it is only for an hour: this will have an effect on your faith, your heart, and your worship, through his blessing.

If someone's words do not go beyond his actions, whose actions do not go beyond his truthfulness, and whose truthfulness does not contend with his Lord, then sit with him with respect and wait for mercy and blessing. Beware of the proof against you, and make his lime in your company pleasant, so that you do not reproach him and lose. Look at him with the eye of God's favor upon him, His selecting him and His honoring him.

# CHAPTER 77
# Advice (*wasiyah*)

The best of advice and the most necessary is that you do not forget your Lord, and that you remember Him always, and do not rebel against Him, and that you should worship Him whether sitting or standing. Do not be dazzled by His blessings and always be grateful to Him. Do not go out from under the protective cover of His mercy, immensity and majesty, lest you go astray and fall into the field of destruction, even if affliction and adversity touch you and the fires of trials burn you. Know that the afflictions He sends are filled with the eternal marks of His honor, and that the trials He inflicts bring about His pleasure and nearness, even though it may be after some time. What blessings there are for the person who has knowledge, and who is granted success therein!

It is related that when someone asked the Messenger of God for advice, he said, 'Never get angry, for anger contains opposition to your Lord. Beware of making excuses, for they contain hidden polytheism. Say your prayers like someone saying farewell, for it contains a link to God and nearness to Him. Be modest before God as you are modest before the righteous among your neighbors, for this contains increased certainty.'

God has gathered up the advice of all our ancestors,

both distant and near, into one single characteristic – precaution (*taqwa*).

In the words of Almighty God:

✡ Certainly We enjoined those who were given the Book before you, and [We enjoin] you too that you should be careful of [your duty]. (4:131)

This is the sum of every sound act of worship: it is by precaution that people reach the high degrees and highest ranks. It is by precaution that people lead a good life with constant companionship.

✡ Surely those who guard [against evil] shall be in gardens and rivers, in the seat of honor with a most powerful King. (54:54-55)

# CHAPTER 78
## Trustful Reliance

---

Trust (*tawakkul*) is a cup sealed with God: none may drink from it or break the seal save the trustful.

It is as God said:

☼ On Allah should the trustful rely. (14:12)

And

☼ On Allah should you rely if you are believers. (5:23)

God made trust the key of belief, and belief the lock of trust. The reality of trust is preferring others to oneself; the root of preferring others is to advance the other person's claim. He who trusts continues to affirm one of two preferences in his trust. If he prefers what is caused (i.e. phenomenal being), he is veiled by it. If he prefers the Causer of the cause of trust (i.e. the Creator, glory be to Him and may He be exalted!), he remains with Him. If you want to be a man of trust and not a man of causes, then say the *takbīr* over your *ruh* five limes, and bid farewell lo all your hopes as death bids farewell to life.

The lowest level of trust is nothing more than placing

your highest aspiration before your own advancement; moreover, you should neither seek for your own portion nor look for what you lack, for either of those things would break the bond of your belief while you are unaware. If you are truly determined to live by one of the marks of the trusting one, and by His trust with respect to one of these two preferences, then cling to this story for support. It is related that one of the men of trust came to one of the Imams and said to him, 'Show me compassion by answering a question about trust.' The Imam knew the man to be of excellent trust and rare scrupulousness, and he saw his sincerity in what he was asking before the man actually put the question. 'Stay where you are and wail with me for awhile,' he told him. While he was formulating his answer a poor man passed by. The Imam put his hand into his pocket and, taking something out, gave it to the poor man. Then he turned to the man who had asked the question and said, 'Come and ask about what you have seen.' 'O Imam,' the man said, '1 know that you could have given me the answer to my question before making me wait. Why then did you delay?' And the Imam replied, 'Belief means reflecting on the meaning before I speak. For how could I be negligent of my innermost being when my Lord perceives it? How could I discuss the science of trust while there is a coin in my pocket? It is not permitted for me to discuss that until after I had given it to him, so understand!' The questioner sighed deeply and swore that he would not seek shelter in a house nor rely on another mortal as long as he lived.

# CHAPTER 79
## Respect for One's Brothers

The reason why brothers in the faith shake hands is God's love for them. The Messenger of God said, 'Whenever brethren shake hands in God, their wrong actions are dispersed so that they become as they were on the day their mothers bore them.' No two brothers' love and respect for each other increases without there being increase for each of them also. It is obligatory for the one having most knowledge of God's faith among the two to stimulate his friend to perform the obligatory functions which God has made necessary, and to guide him in going straight, in contentment and moderation, to give him the good news of God's mercy and to make him fear His punishment. The other brother must seek the blessing of his guidance and hold to what he calls him to, adhere to his admonition, and be guided by him, all the while seeking protection in God and seeking His help and success.

Jesus was once asked, 'How are you this morning?' To which he replied, 'I do not possess the benefit which I hope for, nor can I repel what I am on my guard against, while I am commanded to obey and forbidden to rebel. I do not think that any pauper is poorer than I am.' And when Uways al-Qarani was asked the same question, he said,

'How is a man in the morning when he does not know if he will be alive in the evening, and in the evening he does not know if he will be alive in the morning?' Abu Dharr said, 'In the morning I thank my Lord and I thank myself,' The Prophet said, 'Whoever wakes up in the morning aspiring for something other than God has become among the losers and transgressors.'

# CHAPTER 80
# Striving and Discipline

B liss belongs to the bondsman who strives for God against his own nature and passions: he who then defeats his passion wins God's pleasure, and the one whose intellect leaves behind the self which commands evil through his striving, submission and humility in the service of God has won a great victory. There is no veil between the bondsman and God which is darker or more desolate than that of self and passion; there is no better weapon to fight and destroy them than total need of God, glory be to Him, fear, hunger, thirst in the day and wakefulness at night. When a person possessing these traits dies, he dies a martyr. If he lives according to the straight path, his end will take him to the greatest pleasure of God.

God said:

✿ And [as for] those who strive hard for Us, We will most certainly guide them in our ways, and Allah is most surely with the doers of good. (29:69)

When you see someone striving harder than you, upbraid yourself, and reproach yourself in order to encourage yourself to do more. Put a halter of command

and rein of prohibition on the self, and carry on as if you were a trainer who does not let his mount take a step unless it is completely correct.

The Messenger of God used to pray until his feet were swollen. He would say, 'How can I not be a thankful slave?' The Prophet wanted to make his community consider this so that they would not neglect striving, toil, and discipline in any state. If you were to experience the sweetness of worshipping God, to see its blessing and be illuminated by its light, you would not be patient without it for a single hour, even if you were to be cut to pieces. No one turns away from it without being denied such benefits of protection and success from God as were attained by his forefathers. Rabi` ibn Khuthaym was asked why he did not sleep at night. 'Because I fear to spend the night in sleep,' he replied.

# CHAPTER 81
# Contemplation of Death

Contemplating death kills desire, cuts of the roots of heedlessness and strengthens the heart with God's promise of life hereafter. It refines nature, breaks the signs of passion, extinguishes the fire of greed and renders this world vile; this is the meaning of the Prophet's words: 'To reflect for an hour is better than a year of worship.' That hour of reflecting is the moment when you unite the ropes binding you to this world and fasten them to the next. The descent of mercy from Heaven never ceases when death is remembered in this way. If a person does not reflect on death, and on his own lack of any means to escape it, on his great incapacity, on the length of time he will spend in the grave and his bewilderment at the Resurrection, there is no good in him.

The Prophet said, 'Remember the destroyer of pleasures.' When asked what that was, he replied, 'Death. Whenever one of God's servants remembers this when he is wealthy, this world is constricted for him. Whenever he remembers it in hardship, it is expanded for him.' Death is the first station of the next world and the last station of this world. Blessed is he who shows himself generous and benefits at the beginning, and blessed is he who has done his best at the end.

Death is the closest thing to accompany the son of Adam, although he deems it to be the furthest away. How much man inflicts on himself! What weaker creature is there? In death lies the rescue of the sincere and the destruction of the wrongdoers. That is why some yearn for death yearn for it while others hate it. The Prophet said, 'If a person meets God, God loves to meet him; and if a person hates to meet God, the God hates to meet him.'

# CHAPTER 82
# Good Opinion

The root of good opinion is a man's belief and the soundness of his heart; the sign of good opinion is that whenever he looks, he sees with the eye of purity and virtue wherever he goes, and modesty, trustworthiness, protection and truthfulness are cast into his heart. The Prophet said, 'Have a good opinion of your brothers: through that you will gain purity of heart and firmness of nature.' And Ubayy ibn Ka`b said, 'When you see a quality which you disapprove of in one of your brothers, then give it seventy interpretations and see if your heart can be at peace with one of them. If it is not, then blame yourself if you cannot excuse him. If you yourself have a quality which will easily make for seventy interpretations, then you should disapprove of yourself more than you do of him.' As God revealed to David, 'Remind My slaves of My blessings and My favors. They have only seen exquisite goodness from Me so they should only expect that what remains will be like what they have already had from Me.'

Good opinion invites good worship. A person who is deluded continues to remain in rebellion even while he hopes for forgiveness. The best opinion in God's creation is reserved for those who obey Him, hope for His reward and fear His punishment. The Messenger of God said, relating from his Lord, 'I am with My slave's good opinion of Me, O Muhammad.' Whoever fails to live up to the reality of the gifts which come from his opinion of his Lord has intensified the proof against himself, and is among those who are deceived by the shackles of his passion.

# CHAPTER 83
# Entrusting Oneself to God

He who entrusts his affair to God is in eternal rest and constant carefree ease of life; he is above caring about anything except God, as the Commander of the Faithful said:

☼ I was content with what God allotted me,

☼ and I entrusted my affair to my Creator.

☼ As God was good in what has passed,

☼ so He will be good in what remains.

As God said, in the words of a believer among the people of Pharaoh:

☼ "I entrust my affair to Allah, surely Allah sees the servants". So Allah protected him from the evil consequences of what they planned and the most evil punishment overtook Pharaoh's people. (40:44-45)

The Arabic word for entrustment (*tafwīd*) consists of five letters, each letter having an injunction. He who heeds their commands brings the *ta'* of his abandoning (*tark*) plans in this world; the *fa'* of the annihilation (*fana'*) of every aspiration other than God; the *waw* of fulfilling (*wafa'*) the contract and confirming the promise; the *ya'* of despairing (*ya's*) of yourself, and certainty (*yaqīn*) in your Lord; and the *dad* of a conscience (*damir*)[14] which is purely for God, and of the need (*darurah*) for Him. He who entrusts everything to God wakes up in the morning free of all evils, and at night sleeps protected in his faith.

---

14      *damir* can also be spelled as *zameer*. So this statement can also be written as '*zaz* of a consciousness (*zameer*)'.

# CHAPTER 84
## Certainty

Certainty will take the bondsman to every sublime state and every wondrous station; thus did the Messenger of God make known the immensity of certainty when he mentioned that Jesus walked on water. He said, 'If he had had more certainty, he could have walked on air.' By this he indicated that in spite of the majesty of the place which the prophets have with God, they also have different ranks according to their certainty. Certainty is ever-increasing, and remains so throughout eternity.

Believers also vary in the strength and weakness of their certainty. A person whose certainty is strong may be recognized by the fact that he finds himself stripped of all ability and power other than what God has given him, and by his keeping to God's command and worship both outwardly and inwardly. He considers the states of having and not having, increase and decrease, praise and blame, might and abasement, all to be the same because he considers them all on an equal level. However, a person who weakens his certainty attaches himself to external matters, and allows his self free rein therein. He follows the customs and sayings of people without substantiating them, and strives in the affairs of this world, accumulating its wealth and holding on to it, acknowledging and affirming it with his tongue. There is no withholder or giver except God, and the slave can only obtain what he is provided with and allotted. Effort will not increase provision, but he disavows that by his action and his heart.

In God's words:

☼ They say with their mouths what is not in their hearts; and Allah best knows what they conceal. (3:167)

God was compassionate to His bondsmen when He gave them permission to earn money however they might as long as they do not exceed the limits of God or abandon their obligations to Him and the behavior of His Prophet in any of their actions, or abandon the spirit of trust or become caught in the field of greed. But when they forget this, attaching themselves to the opposite of what has been delineated for them, they are counted among the destroyed, who at the end have nothing but false claims. Not everyone who earns is necessarily trustful: from his earnings he brings for himself only what is forbidden or doubtful. He may be recognized by the effect his gains have upon him, by his insatiable hunger, and how he spends for this world without let.

He who is given permission to earn is one whose self gains while his heart trusts in God. If he has a lot of money, he is like a trustee who knows that having property and not having it is the same thing. If he withholds it, he withholds for God; and if he spends it, he does so in the way God has commanded. Both are for God.

# CHAPTER 85
## Fear and Hope

Fear is the custodian of the heart, and hope is the intercessor of the self; whoever knows God fears Him and sets his hopes in Him. They are the wings of belief with which the true servant flies to God's pleasure. They are the eyes of his intellect, with which he sees God's promise and threat; fear contemplates the justice of God through careful awareness of that threat. Hope calls for God's overflowing favor and gives life to the heart, while fear kills the self. The Messenger of God said, 'The believer has two kinds of fear: fear of what has passed and fear of what is to come.'

In the death of the self lies the life of the heart, which leads to firmness in practice. Whoever worships God with a balance of fear and hope will not be misguided, and will obtain what he hopes for. How can a slave be anything other than fearful when he does not know at what action his record will be closed, while he has to his credit no deed capable of helping him, no power to do anything, nor any place to fly to? How can he fail to hope when he knows that despite his incapacity he is drowned in the seas of God's blessings and favors, which cannot be counted or numbered? The lover worships his Lord with hope by contemplating his own state with the eye of wakefulness; and the abstinent worships with fear.

Uways al-Qarani said to Haram ibn Hayyan, 'People act in hope.' 'But you act in fear,' Haram replied. There are two types of fear: permanent and changing. Permanent fear brings about hope, while changing fear brings about permanent fear. Similarly, there are two types of hopes; concealed and open. Concealed hope brings about permanent fear, which strengthens the connection of love; while open hope fulfils a man's expectations regarding his incapacity and shortcomings in the things he has done during his life.

# CHAPTER 86
## Contentment

Contentment is when a person is content with what he loves and what he hates; it is a ray of the light of gnosis. He who is content is annihilated to all his choices; he is really the one with whom God is content. Contentment is a name which contains the meanings of servitude, and maybe described as the joy of the heart.

I heard my father, Muhammad al-Baqir, say, 'To attach the heart to what is present is association (*shirk*), and to what is not there is disbelief (*kufr*): these are the wings of heedlessness.' I am amazed at anyone who claims to be a slave to God and then contends with Him over His decrees. Content gnostics (*`ārifīn*) are far from being like that.'

# CHAPTER 87
## Affliction

---

Affliction is an adornment for the believer and a mark of honor for the man of intellect, because facing it directly needs steadfastness and firm-footedness, both of which confirm belief. The Prophet said, 'We, the company of the prophets, are the people who have the hardest trials, then after us come the believers, then the others like them.'

Whoever tastes the food of affliction while under God's protection enjoys it more than he enjoys God's blessing. He yearns for it when it is not there, because the lights of blessing lie under the balance of affliction and trial, and the balance of affliction and trial lies under the lights of blessing. Many are delivered from affliction and then destroyed in blessing. God praised none of His bondsmen, from Adam up to Muhammad, until He had tested him and seen how he fulfilled the duty of worship while in affliction. God's marks of honor come, in fact, at the last stage, but the afflictions themselves come in the beginning.

Whoever leaves the path of affliction is ignoring the lamp of the believers, the beacon of those near to God, and the guide for those on the right path. There is no good in a slave who complains of a single trial preceded by thousands of blessings and followed by thousands of comforts. Whoever does not show the patience required in affliction is deprived of thankfulness in the blessings he receives. Similarly, whoever does not give the thankfulness owed for blessings is denied the patience owed in affliction. Whoever is denied both of them is an outcast.

Ayyub said in his supplication, 'O God, verily seventy comforts and ease did not come to me until You sent me seventy afflictions.' And Wahb ibn Munabbih said, 'Affliction to a believer is like a bit to a horse and a halter to a camel.' `Ali said, 'Steadfastness in relation to belief is like the head to the body. The head of steadfastness is affliction, but only those who act righteously understand that.'

# CHAPTER 88
## Patience

Patience[15] reveals whatever light and purity there is in the innermost being of God's servants, while anxiety shows up the darkness and bereftness inside them. Everyone claims to be patient, but only the humble are firm in it. Everyone denies his anxiety, although it is quite obvious in a hypocrite because the onset of trials and afflictions tells you who is truthful and who is a liar.

Patience is a sensation which continuously prevails in one's consciousness, but what occurs upon a sudden upset cannot be called patience. Anxiety is what disturbs the heart and brings the person sorrow, changing his complexion and his state. Every event whose beginnings are without humility, repentance, and humble supplication to God comes from someone who is anxious, not someone who is patient. The beginning of patience is bitter, but its end is sweet for some people; but for others both its beginning and end are bitter. Whoever enters it at its end has entered

---

15     COMMENT: Being patient is like freezing time. Patience is a mark of submission: if you submit fully, you go to the end of the matter. By being patient, you reduce the period of waiting, as it were, to zero time. As far as the matter, in regard to which patience is being called for, is concerned, time and the very existence of the matter ceases to have any bearing on the individual. Shaykh Fadhlalla Haeri.

it. Whoever enters it from its beginning has left it. A person who knows the value of patience cannot bear to be without it.

In the story of Moses and Khidr God said:

✿ How can you have patience in that of which you have no comprehensive knowledge? (18:68)

Whoever is unwillingly patient, who does not complain to people and does not become anxious when his veil is rent, is counted among the common people. His share is as God said:

✿ Give good news to the patient, (2:155)

that is, good news of the Garden and forgiveness. Whoever meets affliction with an open heart, showing patience with tranquility and dignity, is counted among the elite and his portion is as God said:

✿ Surely Allah is with the patient. (8:46)

# CHAPTER 89
## Sorrow

Sorrow[16] is one of the marks of the gnostics, through the magnitude of what comes to them of the Unseen when they are in seclusion, and the intensity of their glorification of God. The outer being of the sorrowful is contraction and his inner being is expansion. He lives with men contentedly, in a life of nearness to God. The sorrowful person is not a man of reflection, because he who reflects is forced to do so, while a sorrowful person is so by nature. Sorrow comes from within, and reflection begins by seeing phenomena – there is a difference between them.

God said in the story of Jacob:

✿ I only complain of my grief and sorrow to Allah, and I know [from Allah] what you do not know. (12:86)

---

16    COMMENT: Sorrow (*huzn*) is a state in which, by being aware, one is not forgetful, nor is one overwhelmed by pleasures and emotions. *Huzn* brings about awareness that the end is close, and therefore it is the foundation of wisdom. Because sorrow is based on the knowledge of the nature of the world, it tethers emotionality and false expectation. It is a spiritual door for inner enlightenment. Shaykh Fadhlalla Haeri.

THE LANTERN OF THE PATH

This is because the knowledge gained in the state of sorrow is particular to him, and God has singled him out for it and left the rest of the world deprived. When Rabi` ibn Khuthaym was asked why he was sorrowful, he replied, 'Because I have demands made on me. At the right of sorrow stands contrition, and at the left of it stands silence. Sorrow is a mark of the gnostics of God.'

Reflection is shared by both the elite and the common folk. If sorrow were to be veiled from the hearts of the gnostics for an hour, they would have to seek for help; but if it were to be placed in the hearts of others, they would dislike it. Sorrow is first, while second come security and good news. Reflection comes second, following the establishment of one's belief in and utter need of God by one's seeking rescue with Him. The sorrowful person reflects, and he who reflects takes note. Each of them has a state, a science, a path, forbearance and honor.

# CHAPTER 90
## Modesty

Modesty is a light whose essence is the heart of belief, meaning careful consideration in everything which is denounced by *tawhīd* and gnosis. The Prophet said, 'Modesty is part of belief.' That is to say, modesty is accepted through belief, and belief is accepted through modesty. The modest person is all good. Whoever is denied modesty is all evil, even if he worships and is scrupulous. One step taken with modesty in the courtyards of God's awe is better than seventy years of worship. Insolence, however, is the beginning of hypocrisy, schism and disbelief.

The Messenger of God said, 'If you have no shame, then do as you like.' This means that when modesty leaves you, then you are punished for all the good or evil that you do. The strength of modesty comes from sorrow and fear, and modesty is the home of fear. The beginning of modesty is awe, and its end is clear vision. A modest person is occupied with his own affairs, withdrawn from people, and distant from what they are doing, even if they all forsake completely person with modesty.

The Messenger of God said, 'When God desires good for a bondsman, he makes him forget his good qualities, putting his evil qualities before his eyes and making him dislike sitting with those who turn away from the remembrance of God.' Modesty is of five kinds: shame for a wrong action; shame for one's incapacity; modesty in the face of a noble equality; the modesty of love, and the modesty of awe. Each of these has its adherents, who are ranked according to these categories of modesty.

# CHAPTER 91
# Gnosis (*ma`rifah*)

The person of the gnostic (*`ārif*) is with the people, while his heart is with God. If his heart were to forget God for the time it takes to blink an eye, he would die of yearning for Him. The gnostic is the trustee over the happenings of God, the treasury of His secrets, the repository of his lights, the proof of His mercy to creation, the instrument of His sciences and the measure of His favor and justice. He needs neither people, nor a goal, nor this world. He has no intimate except God, nor any speech, gesture or breath except by God, with God, and from God, for he frequents the garden of His sanctity and is enriched by His subtlest favors to him. Gnosis is a root whose branch is belief.

# CHAPTER 92
## Love of God

When love of God takes possession of the innermost being of God's bondsman, it empties him of every preoccupation except remembrance of God. The lover is the most inwardly sincere of all people for God. He is the most truthful in his words, the most faithful in his pledge, the most astute in his actions, the purest in remembrance, and the greatest in devoting his self in worship. The angels compete with each other to converse with him, and boast of having seen him. Through him God makes His lands flourish, and by His regard, God honors His slaves. God gives to people when they ask Him by His right, and removes afflictions from them by His mercy. If people knew how they stand with God, they would not try to draw near to God save by the dust of his feet.

The Commander of the Faithful said, 'Love of God is a fire which does not pass by anything without burning it up; the light of God does not come over something without illuminating it. The skies of God do not cause a cloud to appear without it covering whatever is beneath it; the wind of God does not blow on something without it moving. God's water gives life to everything, and from God's earth everything grows. Whoever loves God is given every possession and authority.'

The Prophet said, 'When God loves a slave in my community, He casts love of him into the hearts of His friends, the spirits of the angels and the keepers of His throne,[17] so that they love him. That lover truly has an abundance of bliss, and will be able to intercede with God on the Day of Resurrection.'

---

17 cf. Qur'an 69:17.

# CHAPTER 93
# Love for the Sake of God

He who loves for the sake of God is beloved of God, and he who is loved for the sake of God is also beloved of God, since each loves the other for the sake of God. The Messenger of God said, 'Man is with whom he loves. Whoever loves a bondsman in God, loves God. No one loves God except he whom God loves.' And again, 'The best of people after the prophets in this world and the next are those who love each other for God.' Every love based on some cause other than God brings about enmity except for these two, for they come from the same source. Theirs always increases and never decreases.

As God said:

&#9788; The friends shall on that day be enemies to one another except for those who guard against evil. (43:67)

because the root of love is being free of everything except the Beloved.

The Commander of the Faithful said, 'The best thing in the Garden and the sweetest is love of God, love in God, and praise for God.'

And God has said:

✧  The last of their supplication shall be "Praise be to Allah, Lord of the worlds", (10:10)

because when they see the blessings that exist in the Garden, love is aroused in their hearts and then they call out, 'Praise be to God, Lord of the worlds.'

# CHAPTER 94
## Yearning

He who yearns neither desires food, nor finds pleasure in drink, nor is he quickly excitable, nor is he intimate even with his close friends, nor does he seek refuge in a house, nor does he dwell in a city, nor wear a garment nor take rest enough for his need. He worships God night and day, hoping to reach the object of his yearning. He speaks to Him with the tongue of yearning, declaring what is in his innermost being. This is as God said of Moses when he met his Lord:

> ☼ I hastened to you, my Lord, that You might be pleased. (20:84)

The Prophet explained his state as follows: 'He neither ate, drank, slept nor desired any of that in his coming or going for forty days, out of his yearning for his Lord.'

When you enter the arena of yearning, then say *takbīr* for yourself and your desires in this world. Bid farewell to all familiar things, and turn from all except the One you desire most. Say the word *Labbayk* ('At Your service') between your life and your death: 'At Your service, O God, at Your service!' Then God will make your reward great. A person who yearns is like a drowning man: he is only concerned with being saved, and forgets everything else.

# CHAPTER 95
# Wisdom

Wisdom is the light of gnosis, the measure of fearful awareness and the fruit of truthfulness. God has not given any of his servants a greater, more favorable, generous, lofty or more splendid blessing than wisdom for the heart. In God's words:

> ✿ He grants wisdom to whom He pleases and whoever is granted wisdom, he indeed is given a great good and none but those of understanding remember. (2:269)

That is, only the one whom I have singled out for My sake and whom I have designated for it knows what wisdom I have reserved and prepared. Wisdom is rescue, steadiness at the beginning of the affair and a firm stance at the end. It makes God's creatures aspire to Him. And the Messenger of God said to `Ali, 'That God should guide one of His slaves at your hands is better for you than everything the sun shines upon, from east to west.'

# CHAPTER 96
## Making Claims

In reality the claim belongs to the prophets, the Imams and the truthful, and a man who makes a claim improperly is like the accursed Iblis. He lays claim to devoutness while in reality he contends with his Lord and opposes His command. Whoever makes such claims reveals his lie, and the liar is not trustworthy; whoever claims what is not lawful for him has the gates of affliction opened for him. Anyone who makes a claim will doubtless be asked for clear proof, upon which he is shown to be bankrupt and disgraced. The truthful person is not asked the reason for his actions; as `Ali said, 'No one sees a truthful person without being in awe of him.'

# CHAPTER 97
## Taking Heed

---

The Messenger of God said, 'He who learns his lessons in this world lives in it like a man asleep: he sees it but does not touch it. Abhorrence is increased in his heart and in his self by the behavior of those who are deceived by this world, which can only bring the reckoning and punishment. He exchanges that world for what will bring him near to God's pleasure and pardon. He washes himself free of those things to which the world invites him, and of its worldly adornments, with the water of the world's extinction.

Taking heed brings three things to the person who does so: knowledge of what he does, acting by what he knows, and knowledge of what he does not know. The root of taking heed lies in one's fear of its outcome, when he sees that he has fully realized abstinence at the beginning. Taking heed is only successful for those who have purity and insight.

God said:

✿ Take a lesson, O you who have eyes! (59:2)

And again:

✿ For surely it is not the eyes that are blind, but blind are the hearts which are in the breasts. (22:46)

When God opens the eye of someone's heart and insight by means of consideration, then He has given him a high station and an immense fortune.

# CHAPTER 98
# Contentedness

If a man of contentedness were to swear that he would eventually be in charge of his two abodes, God would confirm him in that, realizing his hope through the immensity of his contentment. How can God's servant not be content with what He has allotted him when

He says:

☼ We distribute among them their livelihood between them in the life of this world. (43:32)

Whoever yields to God, and is not heedless in affirming Him in what He wishes and whenever He wishes, whoever has certainty of His lordship ascribes of necessity the allotment of each man's provision directly to Himself, and does not recognize the reality of causes. Whoever is content with what is allotted is relieved of care, grief and fatigue. Whenever he decreases in contentment, he increases in desire. Greed for this world is the root of every evil; the person who has it is not saved from the Fire unless he repents.

That is why the Prophet said, 'Contentment is a kingdom which does not vanish.' It is the ship of God's pleasure, bearing whoever is on board it to His House. Have excellent trust in what you have not been given, and pleasure in what you have been given. Be patient in what befalls you, for this indeed is one of the greatest tasks.

# CHAPTER 99
## Slander

Slander is forbidden to all Muslims, and he who slanders has sinned in every instance. Slander is when you mention something about a person which is not a fault in God's eyes, or when you censure what the people of knowledge praise.

As for discussing someone who is not present with regard to something which God censures, when that person is guilty of it, then this does not amount to slander, even if he dislikes it when he hears it; and you are free of any slight of that person. This is in order to make the truth clear from the false by the clarification of God and His Messenger. However, this has a precondition, in that the person who says it must seek only to clarify what is true and false, in the faith of God. If he means to deprecate the person of whom he talks without meaning to make things clear, then he is taken to task for his corrupt goal, even if he is correct in what he says.

If you really slander someone, then seek pardon from that person. If you do not go that far nor reach that point, then ask God's forgiveness for that. Slander eats up good deeds as fire eats up wood. As God revealed to Moses, 'The slanderer will be the last to enter the Garden, if he repents. If he does not repent, then he will be the first to enter the

Fire.'

As He said:

✿ Does one of you like to eat the flesh of his dead brother? You would hate it. (49:12)

The various aspects of slander occur when you mention a fault in someone's character, intellect, action, behavior, belief, ignorance and so on.

The origin of slander may be one of ten types: venting one's anger, pleasing other people, suspicion, believing a report without investigating it, having a bad opinion, envy, mockery, astonishment at some action in another which one does not comprehend, dissatisfaction or impatience with others, and embellishment of oneself at the expense of others.

If you seek Islam, then remember the Creator and not the created; then the circumstances of slander will be a lesson for you, and a wrong action will be replaced by a reward.

# Glossary of Arabic Terms

*`abd* — bondsman or servant in the service of God

*adab* — courtesy towards one's brother and God

*ahl al-bayt* — the family, household and progeny of the Prophet

*awliya'* — friends or intimates of God

*dīn* — the religion or faith of Islam, and its all-encompassing code for living

*faqr* — poverty and need of God in all circumstances

*halāl* — whatever has been permitted to the believer by God

*harām* — whatever has been forbidden to the believer by God

*himmah* — yearning for God and spiritual determination before action

*huzn* — outer apprehension and inner grief

*`ibādah* — worship; performance of customs and obligations in worship

*jihād* — the struggle in the way of God, both outwardly (for the sake of establishing truth and justice in an unbalanced situation) and inwardly (against the self)

*khashyah* — caution, and fear of God in one's prayer and actions

*mā'rifah* — gnosis, knowledge, cognizance

*nafs* — the self, i.e. the totality of man's senses, desires and past memories, which, if given reality or allowed to solidify, may obscure the clarity of one's heart and its perception by God

*qiblah* — the direction of the Ka'bah, the Sacred House at Makkah

*ri'ayah* — guarding oneself from a wrong action

*rububiyah* — the lordship of God over His servants

*ruku'* — bowing (after the standing position of prayer)

*ruh* — the soul or breath of man, which leaves him at his death

*salām* — peace; the Muslim greeting of peace

*salamah* — well-being, safety, soundness, peace

*shahādah* — bearing witness that God is One and Muhammad is His Messenger

*shirk* — polytheism, associating something else with God, be it in worship of an idol or of some non-material idea or quality

*siwāk* — the green twig of the *arak* tree used by the Prophet as a tooth-stick

*sujud* — prostration to God in prayer

*sunan* (sing. *sunnah*) — the totality of behavioral practices of the Prophet, which are to be emulated by Muslims

*tahajjud* — striving to stand all night in prayer

*takbīr* — the declaration that God is great

*taqwa* — the state of fear and respect of God which precedes eight action; precaution

*tashahhud* — bearing witness (*shahādah*) at the end of each prayer

*taslīm* — making a *salām* to the Prophet at the end of each prayer

*tawakkul* — trustful reliance on God

*tawfīq* — harmony and success by God's will

*tawhīd* — Divine unity; belief in the Oneness of Allah

*'ubudiyah* — the state of bondage in contrast to the state of *rububiyah*

*wasi* — vicegerent; inheritor

*wasiyah* — will; advice and instruction, given, for example, by the Prophet

*wudu`* — ritual purification by water (which precedes the prayer)

*zuhd* — abstaining from something, or not making an excessive effort to acquire something which is not absolutely necessary